my Book

Grade 2

Modules 4-6

Authors and Advisors

Alma Flor Ada • Kylene Beers • F. Isabel Campoy
Joyce Armstrong Carroll • Nathan Clemens
Anne Cunningham • Martha C. Hougen • Tyrone C. Howard
Elena Izquierdo • Carol Jago • Erik Palmer
Robert E. Probst • Shane Templeton • Julie Washington

Contributing Consultants

David Dockterman • Jill Eggleton

Printed in the U.S.A.

ISBN   978-0-358-46151-7

6 7 8 9 10   0868   29 28 27 26 25 24 23 22

4500849307

r1.21

MODULE 4

Once Upon a Time

MODULE 5

Lead the Way

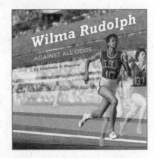

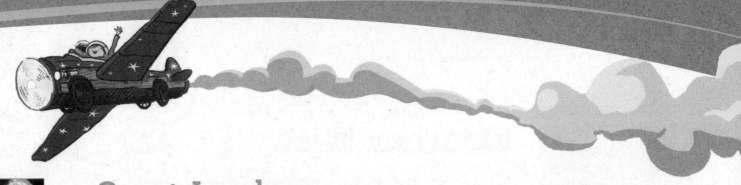

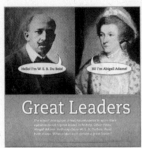

Once Upon a Time

"No book ever ends when
it's full of your friends."

—Roald Dahl

? Essential Question

What lessons can we learn from the characters in stories?

Get Curious Video

Words About Storytelling

Complete the Vocabulary Network to show what you know about the words.

moral

Meaning: A **moral** is a lesson in a story.

Synonyms and Antonyms	Drawing

relate

Meaning: If you **relate** to someone, you know how the person feels.

Synonyms and Antonyms	Drawing

version

Meaning: A **version** is a different or changed form of something.

Synonyms and Antonyms	Drawing

Recipe for a Fairy Tale

You can use a recipe to make breakfast, lunch, or dinner. Can you use one to make a fairy tale, too? Let's find out!

Ingredients

prince

princess

dragon

castle

golden eggs

picnic basket

Directions

1. First, let's do some mixing.

2. Take the castle and the dragon.

3. Add a prince, a princess, and a picnic basket.

4. Now, sprinkle in a little bit of silliness.

5. Stir them all together. What have you got? Read on to find out!

The Story

Once upon a time, a dragon lived all alone in a castle. He never came out or opened the door. The villagers thought he was mean.

One day, a brave prince and a daring princess decided to save their frightened kingdom from the dragon. They marched up to the castle door. The prince hollered, "Open this door, or I'll huff and puff and blow your house down!"

The dragon was very surprised. He peeked out a window and asked, "Really? What if I **do** open the door?"

The princess held up a picnic basket. "Then we can have lunch," she said.

The lonely dragon opened the door. He invited his new friends in for lunch. They all lived happily ever after.

Be the Chef!
What would you mix up for a fairy tale?

Prepare to Read

GENRE STUDY **Procedural texts** tell readers how to do or make something. When you read *How to Read a Story*, notice:

- directions for readers to follow
- main topic and details
- steps that show order
- ways visuals and words help readers understand the text

SET A PURPOSE Read to make smart guesses, or **inferences,** about things the author does not say. Use clues in the text and pictures to help you.

POWER WORDS
cozy
steaming
clue
sense
pause
disturb
rattled
tackled

Meet Kate Messner.

HOW TO
READ
A STORY

by Kate Messner

illustrated by Mark Siegel

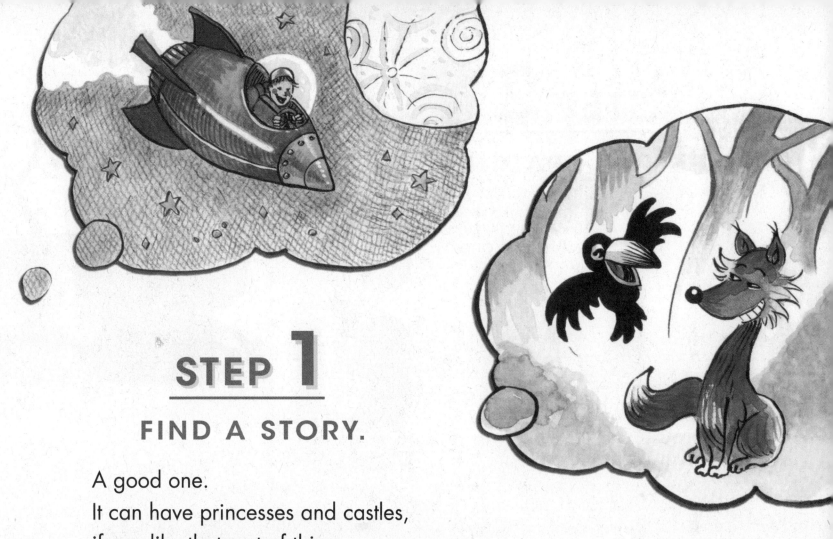

STEP 1

FIND A STORY.

A good one.
It can have princesses and castles,
if you like that sort of thing,
or witches and trolls.
(As long as they're not too scary.)

STEP **2**

FIND A READING BUDDY.

A good one.

A buddy can be older . . .

or younger . . .

or a person your age.

Or maybe not a person at all.

Make sure your reading buddy is nice and snuggly.
And make sure you both like the book.
If you don't agree . . . go back to Step 1.
Sometimes it takes a few tries to find just the right book.

STEP 3

FIND A COZY READING SPOT.

Outside is fun . . . but not if it's very cold.
Unless you have thick woolen blankets,
and hats and scarves, and cups of steaming
hot cocoa.

And not if it's very hot.
Unless you have trees to shade you from
the sun, a hammock to catch cool
breezes, and tall glasses of icy lemonade.

Inside is good.
Couches are cozy. So are chairs
big enough for two.

Just be careful not to get stuck.

STEP 4

LOOK AT THE BOOK'S COVER.

Can you guess what it's about?
Read the title. That might be a clue.

STEP 5

OPEN THE BOOK.

(This is the exciting part!)

Read the story in a loud, clear voice,
not too slow and not too fast.

You can point to words if you like,
but you don't have to do that.

"Once upon a time..."

 **STEP 6** When the characters talk, whatever's being said . . . say it in a voice to match who's talking.

"I will save the kingdom."

"I am the most POWERFUL in all the land!"

"Soon the castle will be MINE."

"I'm hungry for lunch."

"Beep."

STEP 7

No matter what you read, hold the book so your buddy can see the pictures. Buddies get impatient when they can't see well.

STEP 8

If there are words you don't know, try sounding them out or looking at the pictures to see what makes sense.

"They were afraid the dragon would burn down the cass . . . cass . . . Oh . . . The castle!"

They were afraid the dragon would burn down the castle.

If you need a break, you can pause for a minute . . .
and talk to your reading buddy
to predict what might happen next.

THE
PRINCESS

Will the castle catch on fire?
Will the princess tame the dragon?
Will the robot marry the princess?
Will the horse make friends with the dragon?
Will the dragon eat them all for lunch?

STEP 9

When you get to the exciting parts,
make your voice sound exciting, too.

"Who dares disturb me in my cave?" the dragon growled.

"Oh dear! Oh no!"
The robot was so scared all his metal
parts rattled. What would they do?

But the princess tackled that
dragon and held him down.

"You must promise you'll
leave our kingdom in peace!"

When you and your buddy can't stand it a second longer . . .

turn the page to read
how things work out.

STEP 10

When the book is over, say,

"The End."

The dragon promised and decided it was better being friends.

And they all lived happily ever after.

And then . . . if it was a really good story . . .
go right back to the beginning
and start all over again.

Use details from *How to Read a Story* to answer these questions with a partner.

1. **Make Inferences** Why is it important to find just the right book for you and your reading buddy?

2. How are the numbered steps in the text connected? What does the author want you to learn from them?

3. How do you think the author feels about reading? How do you think she wants others to feel about it? Use details from the text to explain your ideas.

Talking Tip

Your ideas are important! Be sure to speak loudly and clearly as you share them.

Write More Steps

PROMPT Think about how following the steps in *How to Read a Story* can help make reading fun. Now think about what makes reading fun for you. What other steps could you add to the text?

PLAN First, draw two steps that you would like to share with others. Be sure they are different from the steps in the text.

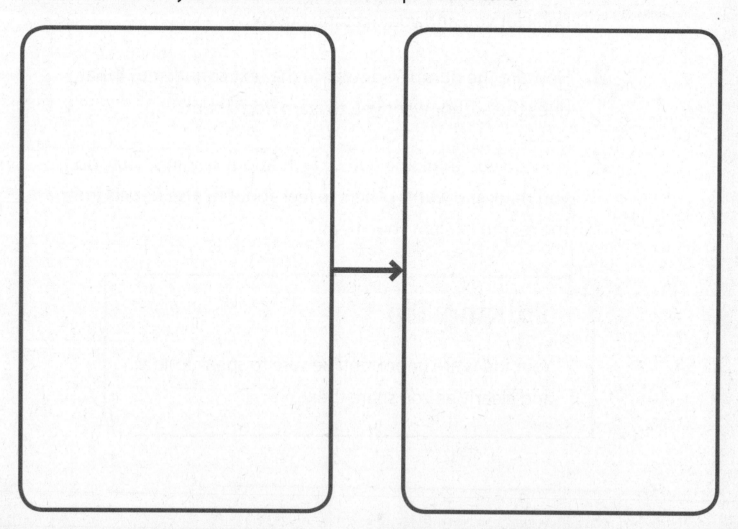

WRITE Now write your own steps to add to *How to Read a Story*. Remember to:

- Choose verbs that tell your readers exactly what to do.

- Use language that will make readers excited about following your steps.

_____

_____

_____

_____

_____

_____

_____

_____

Prepare to Read

GENRE STUDY **Dramas** are plays that are read and performed. As you read *A Crow, a Lion, and a Mouse! Oh, My!,* look for:

- the setting, or where and when the story takes place
- a narrator who reads words the characters do not say
- a list of characters

SET A PURPOSE As you read, **create mental images,** or make pictures in your mind, to help you understand details in the text.

POWER WORDS

plain

bind

narrow

clever

Meet Crystal Hubbard.

A Crow, a Lion, and a Mouse! Oh, My!

two fables retold by Crystal Hubbard

The Lion and the Mouse

CAST: NARRATOR
LION
MOUSE
HUNTER 1
HUNTER 2

NARRATOR On a sunny plain in Kenya, Lion sleeps.

LION **Snoooooore!**

MOUSE (*enters, noisily talking on cell phone*) Have you tasted the new cheeses at the Nairobi Food Mart? They're so good, and they're on sale!

LION (*wakes, grabs Mouse*) I don't like cheeses. I prefer to snack on **meeses!** I mean mice.

MOUSE (*looking fearful*) Please, don't eat me! I'm not even a mouthful. I'm more useful outside your belly than inside.

LION (*yawns*) I'm more sleepy than hungry anyway. Run along, little Mouse. (*falls asleep*)

NARRATOR Sleeping Lion cannot hear danger approach.

HUNTER 1 *(carrying a rope, whispers)* This lion will be our greatest prize!

HUNTER 2 *(helps Hunter 1 bind surprised Lion)* Let's get the truck!

NARRATOR Mighty Lion has a mighty big problem!

MOUSE *(nibbling cheese, drops cheese when he sees Lion)* Dude, what happened?

LION *(looking ashamed)* Hunters trapped me. I'm so embarrassed!

MOUSE Not for long!

NARRATOR Mouse's tiny, sharp teeth chewed and gnawed and tugged at the rope until it fell away.

LION I'm free! *(hugs Mouse)* I learned a lesson today. You're a better friend than a meal! *(Smiling, Lion and Mouse exit together.)*

The Crow and the Pitcher

CAST: `CROW 1`
`CROW 2`
`NARRATOR`

`NARRATOR` On the hottest day of summer, two crows find a pitcher of water.

`CROW 1` *(circling pitcher)* It's half full!

`CROW 2` *(wings crossed over chest)* It's half empty.

`CROW 1` *(tries to stick beak in pitcher)* The opening is too narrow!

`CROW 2` *(tries to lift pitcher)* I can't hold it because I don't have thumbs!

NARRATOR The crows grow thirstier in the heat of the sizzling sun.

CROW 1 *(staring at pitcher)* There has to be a way to get that water.

CROW 2 *(kicking pebble on ground)* I wish I had ice cream. *(kicks a pebble)* Or an ice pop. *(kicks a pebble)*

CROW 1 I've got it! *(picks up a pebble)*

CROW 2 What are you doing with that?

CROW 1 *(drops pebble into pitcher)* You'll see.

35

CROW 2 Are you making Pebble-ade?

CROW 1 (*picks up pebble, drops it in pitcher*) Just keep watching and you'll see how smart I am!

NARRATOR This clever crow can't get to the water, so he's making the water get to him.

CROW 2 (*impressed*) Wow! The water is rising!

CROW 1 (*spits out pebble*) It would rise faster if both of us put in pebbles. (*picks up pebble*)

CROW 2 No, that's okay. You're doing great.

CROW 1 (*drops pebble in pitcher*) There! I can finally get a drink. (*begins sipping water*)

CROW 2 (*behind Crow 1*) Hurry, I want a turn! Save some for me!

Use details from *A Crow, a Lion, and a Mouse! Oh, My!* to answer these questions with a partner.

1. **Create Mental Images** When Mouse sees what happened to Lion, he is so surprised he drops his cheese. What does Mouse see? Use details in the text to help you picture it in your mind. Then describe your picture to a partner.

2. How is the narrator's part different from the other parts in each drama?

3. Why is a fable a good way to teach a lesson? What lessons do you learn from these two fables?

Listening Tip

Look at your partner as you listen. Nod your head to show you are interested.

Write a Thank-You Note

PROMPT How do you think Lion feels about what Mouse did to help him? Use details from the words and pictures to explain your ideas.

PLAN First, add words to the web that describe how you think Lion feels after Mouse helps him.

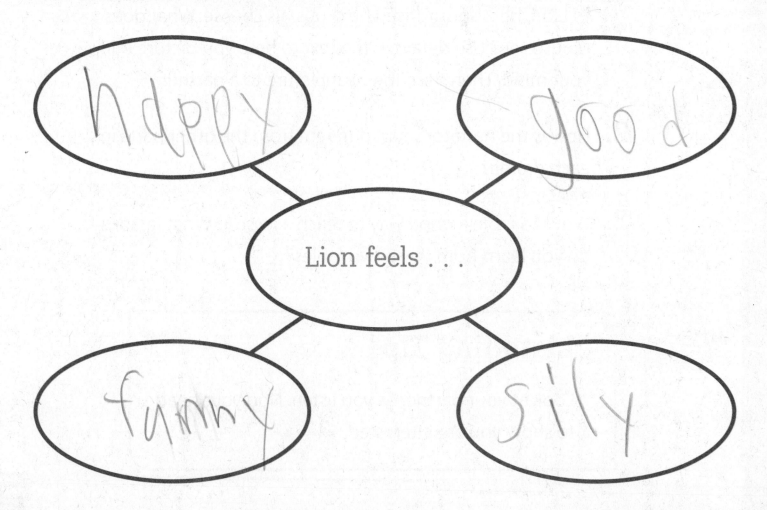

happy

good

Lion feels . . .

funny

sily

WRITE Now write a note from Lion to Mouse thanking him for his help. Remember to:

- Include details from the drama that explain why Lion is thanking Mouse.

- Begin your note with *Dear Mouse*. End it with *Your friend, Lion*.

_____

_____

_____

_____

_____

_____

_____

_____

_____

_____

Prepare to Read

GENRE STUDY **Fantasies** are stories with events that could not really happen. As you read *Hollywood Chicken,* look for:

- animal characters that talk and act like real people
- the beginning, middle, and ending of the story
- problems and solutions

SET A PURPOSE You know that most stories include a problem. Use what you know about the text to make a **prediction,** or good guess, about the problem in this story. Read to see if you are right. If not, make a new prediction.

POWER WORDS

journey

fulfill

believe

speech

Build Background: Hollywood

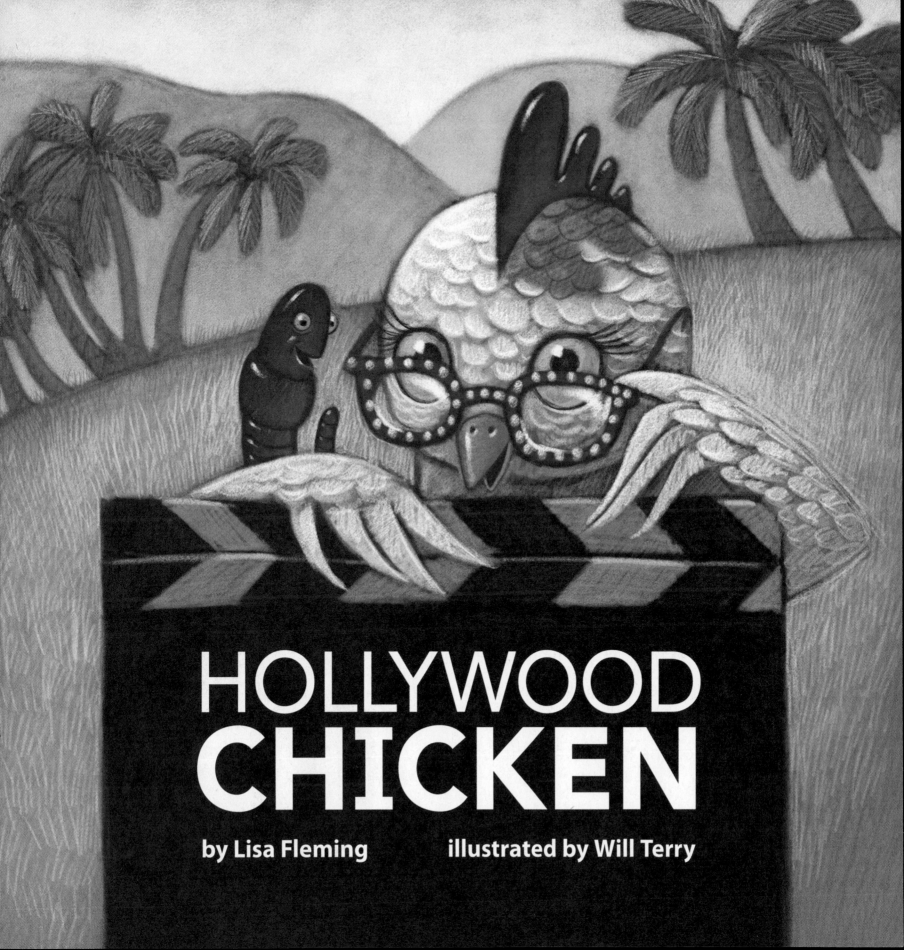

HOLLYWOOD
CHICKEN

by Lisa Fleming   illustrated by Will Terry

Dear Ms. Luz Cruz,

I can't wait to fly this coop! Life in these green hills is dull, dull, dull. The endless farmland, quiet evenings, and the steady diet of corn and more corn just aren't enough for me. I need more from life! How I dream of being on stage! I want to make my way in the city where dreams come true! I could be the next poultry actress to make it big! I, Chicken Lily, will have my own star on the Hollywood Chicken Walk of Fame! Hollywood, here I come!

Sincerely,
Chicken Lily

Starring Chicken Lily

Dear Chicken Lily,
  I am excited to meet you! I am Hollywood's best chicken agent. I will get you parts in movies and help you dream big. I can see your name in lights already! Call me or text me when you get here! 323-555-BOCK
            Kisses,
            Luz Cruz

Ms. Cruz, it's Chicken Lily. I did it! I'm here in Hollywood! My journey was long. I went from the wide green fields of home, over mountains, and through deserts. I had a rough time crossing through the tiny towns filled with homes and cars and people. There was a close call with a cat in Burbank, but I made it!

Oh, the city! It's everything I dreamed it would be! It's big, busy, and beautiful! The buildings are so tall. There are so many people hustling around like squirrels in the fall. Nothing here is like my home on the farm.

Chicken Lily! I am so glad you're here. Get some sleep because you have your first audition in the morning! I know you will knock their socks off! Meet me at my office and we'll go together! Kisses!

45

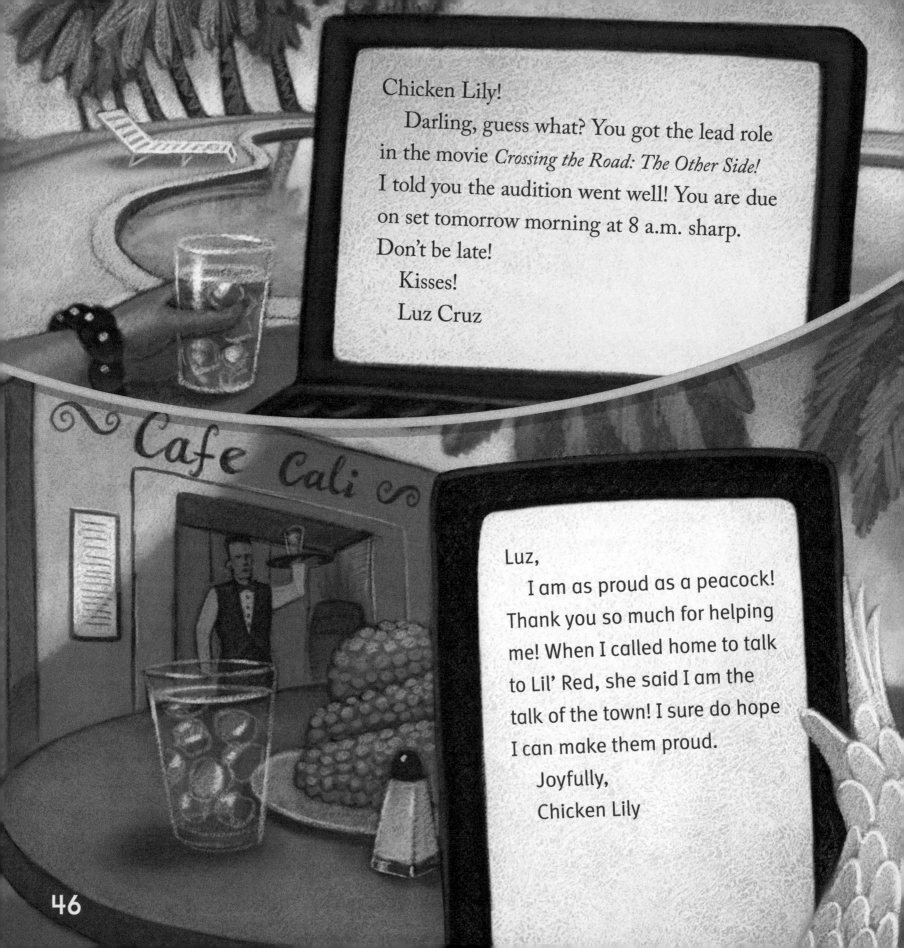

Chicken Lily!

Darling, guess what? You got the lead role in the movie *Crossing the Road: The Other Side!* I told you the audition went well! You are due on set tomorrow morning at 8 a.m. sharp. Don't be late!

Kisses!

Luz Cruz

Luz,

I am as proud as a peacock! Thank you so much for helping me! When I called home to talk to Lil' Red, she said I am the talk of the town! I sure do hope I can make them proud.

Joyfully,

Chicken Lily

Dear Chicken Diary,

Today I got to meet the other actors on my movie. So many of them have gone to big chicken acting schools. A lot have come from families where the chickens all work in the movies. What if I don't fit in?

One of the actors sure made me feel like I don't belong. Slim the Worm made a joke about the way I talk. He didn't think I heard him, but I did.

Did I make the wrong decision when I left the farm? What if I can't fulfill my dream? Maybe I should let Luz Cruz know there is a problem on the set. I don't want her to think I'm as helpless as a chick, though.

Dear Chicken Diary,

Who would believe it? *Crossing the Road: The Other Side* is a smash hit! The movie's success has made me want to work even harder. I started taking a chicken acting class. Every day I meet with my friends to practice my acting skills. I think it is paying off. We start filming *Crossing the Road 2: The Highway* tomorrow!

One thing still bothers me: Slim. He never talks to me on the set. I try to be friendly, but he is always joking around in a way that hurts my feelings. Does he think that I don't belong here? I did talk to Luz about it. She said, "Just talk to him, Chicken Lily! I've worked with him for a long time. You might be worrying about nothing!" I want to talk to him. I'm just scared!

ChickenLily

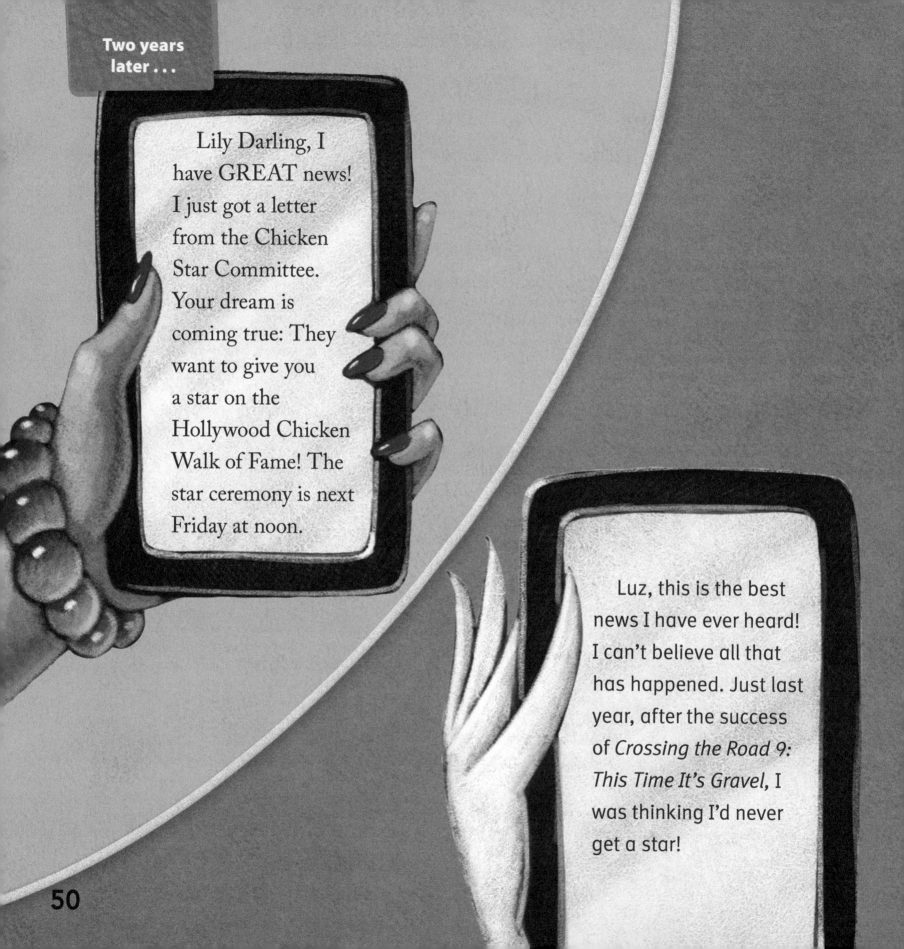

Dear Chicken Diary,

Today was the star ceremony, and it was amazing! I got to give a speech! I also left my chicken footprints in the wet cement on my very own star. My dream came true!

All of my friends from the *Crossing the Road* movies were there. Well, all of them were there except Slim.

51

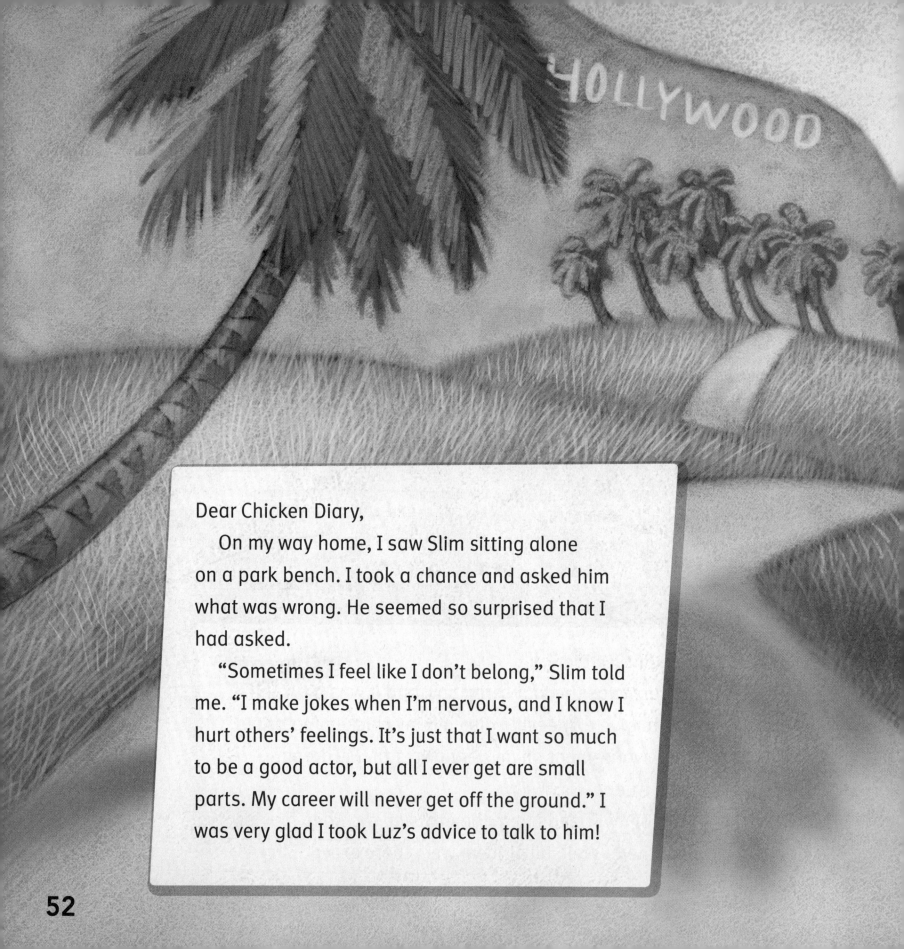

Dear Chicken Diary,

On my way home, I saw Slim sitting alone on a park bench. I took a chance and asked him what was wrong. He seemed so surprised that I had asked.

"Sometimes I feel like I don't belong," Slim told me. "I make jokes when I'm nervous, and I know I hurt others' feelings. It's just that I want so much to be a good actor, but all I ever get are small parts. My career will never get off the ground." I was very glad I took Luz's advice to talk to him!

I put my arm around Slim and told him my story. I told him about my journey from the farm and how I had wondered if I would ever fit in. I told him about my years and years of practice and hard work. And I told him that I would help him make his dreams come true. Maybe some day, my friend Slim might be the first worm to have a star on the Hollywood Chicken Walk of Fame.

Use details from *Hollywood Chicken* to answer these questions with a partner.

1. **Make and Confirm Predictions** What predictions did you make about the problem and resolution before and as you read? What were you right about? What was different?

2. How do the places where Lily lives change in the story? What clues do you see in the pictures about her success?

3. How does Lily feel when she talks to Slim at the end of the story? How does she show her feelings?

Listening Tip

Listen carefully and politely. Look at your partner to show you are paying attention.

Write a Movie Ad

PROMPT Movie ads use words and pictures to get people
excited about seeing a movie. What would a movie ad for
Crossing the Road: The Other Side be like? Look for details in the
words and pictures to help you think of ideas.

PLAN First, think of an exciting scene that might be in the
movie. Draw it. Add the title and the names of the stars.

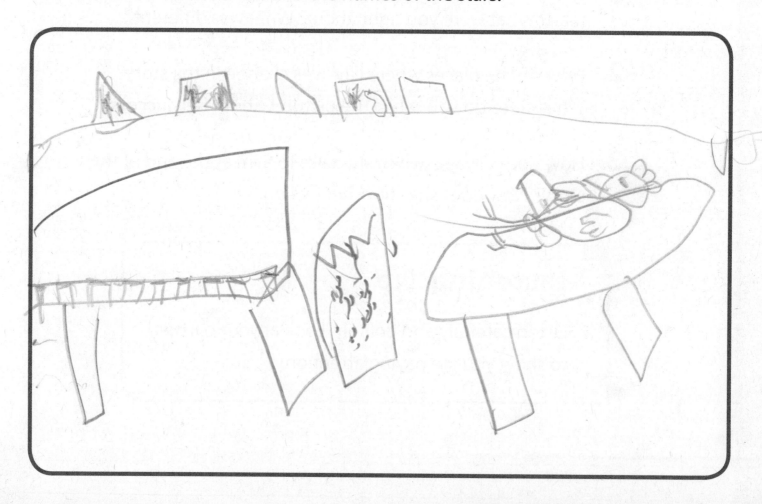

WRITE Now ask yourself what would make you want to see this movie. Write sentences that would persuade other kids to want to see it, too. Remember to:

- Include details about the movie's stars and setting.

- Use describing words such as *greatest*, *silliest*, and *stupendous*.

Beause is good. Bcause
you get free sast.
and free tickis!
Aad you get to
have a free stop
owth ice came cake
sedet.

Prepare to Read

GENRE STUDY **Fairy tales** are old stories with made-up characters and events that could not happen. As you read *If the Shoe Fits: Two Cinderella Stories*, look for:

- clues that the stories are make-believe
- endings that are happy
- problems and solutions

SET A PURPOSE As you read, **make connections** by comparing and contrasting things like characters, setting, or events across the two stories. This will help you understand and remember each text.

POWER WORDS

chore

thrilled

superb

beamed

pleasure

jealous

dashed

hobbled

Meet Pleasant DeSpain.

If the Shoe Fits

Two Cinderella Stories

retold by Pleasant DeSpain

A Cinderella Named Zoey

Once, not long ago, there was a girl named Zoey. She loved school, especially math, PE, and science.

Her stepbrother, Finn, enjoyed playing tricks on Zoey.

One day, their mother tried logging onto her laptop, but her password wasn't accepted.

"Finn, did you change my password?"

"No, Mom. Try Zoey's password."

It worked.

"Zoey!" cried their mother. "You know the rule. You can't use my computer without permission. Instead of going to Randall's party tomorrow, you'll do Finn's chore and mow the lawn."

"But Mom, I didn't . . ."

Laughing, Finn went outside.

Randall had invited all his friends to his birthday party. His mom was baking a delicious chocolate cake. He hoped Zoey would come. She was one of his best friends.

The next day, Finn and their mom left for Randall's party.

The doorbell rang. It was Zoey's favorite neighbor, Mrs. Fortuna. She always sparkled!

"Want to go to the party?"

"How did you know?"

"I have a few secrets, dear."

"But the lawn . . . " began Zoey.

Mrs. Fortuna pulled bright red garden shears from her bag. To Zoey's amazement, the shears flew out of Mrs. Fortuna's hands. The lawn was mowed in seconds.

Zoey was thrilled! She ran to get her favorite shoes, but Finn had hidden them.

"What will I wear?"

Mrs. Fortuna handed her a pair of golden tennis shoes. Zoey thought they were superb!

On the way to Randall's house, one of Zoey's shoes came untied and tumbled onto the street. It was run over by a bus.

"My shoe!" yelled Zoey.

Mrs. Fortuna consoled her. "Two shoes don't make wishes come true."

Randall beamed when Zoey walked in. He invited her to sit next to him. Noticing her one shoe, he thought, "This is something new." Then he said, "Cool, everyone take off one shoe, just like Zoey."

It was time to cut the cake. The candles were lit, and before Randall blew them out, Zoey smiled. One of her wishes had come true.

A Cinderella Named Kwan

A Korean Story

Long, long ago, a baby girl was born. Her father named her Kwan, which means "strong."

Sadly, her mother died.

Years later, Kwan's father remarried. His new wife had her own daughter named Hee, which means "pleasure."

Kwan's stepmother and stepsister were jealous of Kwan and unkind to her.

One beautiful spring morning, Kwan's stepmother said, "I'm taking Hee to the festival."

"Can I go, honorable mother?" asked Kwan.

"Yes, but first you must weed the garden."

Hee and her mother laughed as they left for the city.

Kwan's heart was heavy. The garden was filled with weeds.

She went outside and was surprised by a large brown cow who said, "I'll eat the weeds."

"Yes, please!" Kwan said.

The cow chomped all the weeds in a flash.

Suddenly, a flock of songbirds appeared in the sky, carrying a lovely robe and slippers. "For the strong one," they sang.

Thrilled, Kwan dashed down the road to the bridge crossing the river. She tripped and fell. One of her slippers splashed into the water. "Oh no!" cried Kwan, watching the slipper float away.

Kwan hobbled home and hid the gown and slipper in an old trunk.

Meanwhile, a young prince was traveling to the festival. Thirsty, he stopped by the river for a drink. He put his lips into the cold, rushing water, and a beautiful slipper floated by.

"Pretty slipper, pretty lady?" he asked as he grabbed the slipper.

"Pretty lady," sang the birds flying above.

"I must find her," he declared.

67

The prince traveled to many farms, asking every young woman to try on the slipper. Arriving at Kwan's farm, he showed it to Hee and Kwan.

Hee shoved Kwan to the side, saying, "It's mine!"

"You are not polite," said the prince. "Your sister will try first."

Kwan slipped her foot into the slipper.

"You are strong and beautiful," he said. "Please marry me."

Smiling, Kwan said, "Yes."

The songbirds swirled above. Happy was their song.

Use details from *If the Shoe Fits: Two Cinderella Stories* to answer these questions with a partner.

1. **Make Connections** Compare and contrast the two fairy tales. How are they alike and different?

2. Mrs. Fortuna consoles Zoey when she loses her shoe. Think about a time when you lost something. What made you feel better?

3. If Mrs. Fortuna and the songbirds had not been in the fairy tales, how else could the girls have solved their problems?

Talking Tip

Complete the sentence to add to what your partner says.

My idea is _____.

Write a Comparison

PROMPT Shoes are an important part of both stories. Compare Zoey's shoes with Kwan's shoes. How are their parts in the stories alike? How are they different?

PLAN First, make a list of details about Zoey's shoes. Then, make a list of details about Kwan's shoes. Look for details in the text and illustrations about how they look, where they come from, and what happens to them.

Zoey's shoes	Kwan's shoes

WRITE Now write sentences comparing Zoey's and Kwan's shoes. Use the details in your chart to explain how they are alike and different. Remember to:

- Describe how Zoey and Kwan feel about their shoes.

- Add an apostrophe to show ownership, like *Kwan's shoes*.

_____

_____

_____

_____

_____

_____

_____

_____

_____

_____

Prepare to View

GENRE STUDY **Videos** are short movies that give you information or something for you to watch for enjoyment. As you watch *Those Clever Crows*, notice:

- how pictures, sounds, and words work together
- what the video is about
- information about the topic
- the tone or mood of the video

SET A PURPOSE Ask yourself what happens and why to make **cause and effect** connections about the video. A cause is something that makes something else happen. An effect is what happens because of the cause.

Build Background: Crows

THOSE CLEVER CROWS

from *The New York Times*

As You View Are crows clever? You decide! Watch the crows' behavior. Think carefully about how the words help you understand what the crows are doing. What do you think those crows must be thinking?

Turn and Talk

THOSE
CLEVER
CROWS
from The New York Times

Use details from *Those Clever Crows* to answer these questions with a partner.

1. **Cause and Effect** What do the crows want to make happen? How do their actions help them reach their goal?

2. How are the crows in the video like the crows in the fable? How are they different?

3. Do you think *Those Clever Crows* is a good title for this video? Use details from the video to explain your ideas.

Talking Tip

Wait for your turn to speak. Talk about your feelings and ideas clearly.

I feel that _____.

Let's Wrap Up!

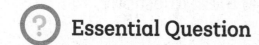 **Essential Question**

What lessons can we learn from the characters in stories?

Pick one of these activities to show what you have learned about the topic.

1. Learn Your Lesson

Think of a lesson that kids can use in their everyday lives. Then write your own fable or fairy tale that teaches that lesson. Look back at the texts for ideas. See how many of those characters you can include in your new story!

2. Story Catalog

Make a catalog of things fables or fairy tales need. Look back at the texts for ideas. Then draw pictures of characters, settings, or objects you might find in those kinds of stories. Label each picture.

Word Challenge

Can you use the word moral in your catalog?

My Notes

Lead the Way

"Great leaders have to think
outside the box sometimes."

—Rick Riordan

? Essential Question

What are the qualities of a good leader?

Get Curious Video

Words About Leadership

Complete the Vocabulary Network to show what you know about the words.

admire

Meaning: When you **admire** someone, you like and respect that person.

Synonyms and Antonyms	Drawing

inspire

Meaning: When people **inspire** you, they give you new ideas.

Synonyms and Antonyms	Drawing

pioneer

Meaning: When you **pioneer** something, you are the first person to do it.

Synonyms and Antonyms	Drawing

What's Good to Read?

Book Reviews for Kids by Kids!

Book: *Emmanuel Ofosu Yeboah: What Makes a Great Leader?* by Malikah Hansen

Genre: Biography

Reviewer: Ruthie Miller

Age: 8

WHAT MAKES A GREAT LEADER?

I think this biography is terrific! It is about a man from Ghana whose leg didn't form properly before he was born. Many people thought he would have a hard life because of his leg. He proved them wrong and became a leader!

I like this book because it shows what happens when people believe in themselves. For example, some people said Emmanuel wouldn't be able to do things like go to school or play sports. Emmanuel had other ideas. He hopped to and from school each day. He learned to play soccer and how to ride a bike.

Another thing I like about the book is that it is about a special kind of leader. Emmanuel set an example for others. He changed how they think. In 2001, Emmanuel rode his bike across Ghana. He showed that people with disabilities can do amazing things.

This book reminds you that everyone is special and can become a leader just like Emmanuel did. Everyone should read it!

Prepare to Read

GENRE STUDY **Fantasies** are stories with made-up events that could not really happen. As you read *Going Places*, look for:

- events that could not happen in real life
- how pictures and words help you understand what happens
- a lesson the main character learns
- problems (conflicts) and solutions (resolutions)

SET A PURPOSE **Ask questions** before, during, and after you read to help you get information or understand the text. Look for evidence in the text and pictures to **answer** your questions.

POWER WORDS

assured

exactly

precise

peered

respond

intent

contraption

replica

Meet Paul A. Reynolds and Peter H. Reynolds.

Going Places

by Peter and Paul Reynolds

illustrated by Peter Reynolds

Rafael had been waiting all year long for the **Going Places** contest, a chance to build a go-cart, race it . . . and win.

When their teacher announced, "Who would like the first kit?" Rafael's hand shot up.

The rest of the class watched enviously as Rafael walked back to his seat with a kit.

Mrs. Chanda assured them, "Don't worry—you'll all be getting one...

"...and they're all EXACTLY alike."

The kit came with a set of precise instructions. That made Rafael happy. He was very good at following directions.

Rafael hammered, glued, nailed, and assembled his kit.

His go-cart looked just like the one in the directions. He was feeling quite proud.

Rafael wondered how his classmate Maya was doing. She lived right next door.

He peered over the fence. "Hey, Maya,
you haven't even started?!"

Maya didn't respond. She was
so intent on watching the bird in
front of her, and quickly sketching it,
that she didn't even notice Rafael.

Then she just put down her pencil
and stared at the bird dreamily.

Rafael shrugged—and let her be.

92

The next morning
Rafael checked back in to
see how Maya was doing.

"Wow, what is that?"
he asked.

Maya grinned. "You
like it?"

Rafael responded slowly, "Yeeeaah—extremely
cool. But, uh, Maya, there's just one little
problem. That's not a go-cart."

Maya smiled. "Who said it HAD to be a go-cart?"

Rafael was confused. The set of instructions inside the box were for a GO-CART. But then again, they didn't say it HAD to be a go-cart. He looked again at Maya's contraption. After a moment, he grinned.

"I get it. Hey, Maya, I really want to win this race. The instructions never said we couldn't team up either!"

And so they did, working late into the evening.

The next day everyone gathered for the big race.
Each go-cart was a perfect replica of the other.

Except one.

One of the kids laughed. "Looks like you had trouble with the **Going Places** instructions. You're going places all right—you're GOING to lose!"

Maya and Rafael didn't even have time to
respond because the announcer's big, boomy
voice called out,

ATTENTION RACERS!
START YOUR ENGINES!
4...3...2...1...

A buzzer sounded.

"And they're off!"

While all the other go-carts disappeared in a cloud of dust, Maya just sat there in their motionless vehicle. Rafael shouted over the roar of engines and cheering crowds. "Maya! What are we waiting for?"

"No worries, Rafael!" Maya answered. "Flaps down, throttle up!"

And now THEY took off—off into the air!

The other contestants looked up in amazement.

Maya and Rafael hovered and then sped past them all.

Before long, Maya and Rafael
coasted across the finish line to the
cheers of the waiting crowd.

They kept rolling clear across the race grounds.
Maya slammed the brakes, stopping just short
of the lake at the edge of the school field.

Rafael noticed a startled frog leap from a lily
pad and dive into the water. He raised his eyebrow
and looked at Maya. She smiled.

"Rafael, are you thinking
what I'm thinking . . . ?"

Rafael just nodded.

Turn and Talk

Use details from *Going Places* to answer these questions with a partner.

1. **Ask and Answer Questions** What questions did you ask yourself about the story before, during, and after reading? How did your questions help you understand the story?

2. Why do the kids laugh when they first see Rafael and Maya's vehicle? How do their feelings change after the race begins?

3. What do you think Rafael learns from this experience?

Talking Tip

Ask a question if you are not sure about your partner's ideas.

Why did you say _____?

Write a Victory Speech

PROMPT What would Maya and Rafael say in a victory speech after the race? Look for details in the words and pictures about how they won and how it makes them feel.

PLAN First, write three details that explain why Maya and Rafael won the race.

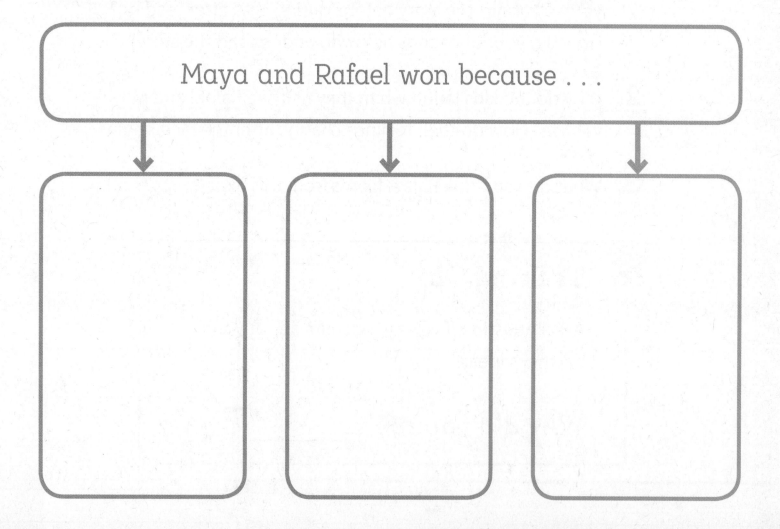

Maya and Rafael won because . . .

WRITE Now use what you know about Maya and Rafael to write their victory speech. Remember to:

- Include exciting details from the race.

- At the end, thank the audience for listening.

_____

_____

_____

_____

_____

_____

_____

_____

_____

_____

Prepare to Read

GENRE STUDY **Biographies** tell about real people's lives. As you read *Wilma Rudolph: Against All Odds*, notice:

- what the person did
- photos of the person
- a timeline that shows order of events

SET A PURPOSE As you read, **summarize** the text. Use your own words to retell the central idea and the relevant details in an order that makes sense.

POWER WORDS

rare

relay

honored

success

Build Background: The Olympics: Track and Field Events

Wilma Rudolph

AGAINST ALL ODDS

by Stephanie E. Macceca

Little Wilma

Wilma Rudolph was born on June 23, 1940, in Tennessee (ten-uh-SEE). She was born early. She only weighed 4.5 pounds. She was often sick because she was so small.

Tennessee

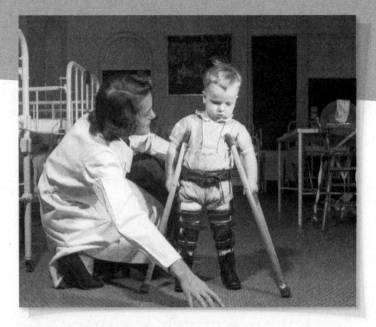

Some children with polio learn to walk with braces and crutches.

President Franklin D. Roosevelt had polio. He could not walk. Today polio is very rare. People can get shots so they do not get polio.

Polio

At age four, Wilma was very sick. She got better. But, her mother was still worried. Something was wrong with her left leg and foot. The doctor said Wilma had polio (POH-lee-oh).

The doctor said Wilma would never walk. Wilma could not walk for two years. Her brothers and sisters helped her by exercising her left foot and leg.

Wilma wore a brace on her leg. She could not play games and sports at school. She watched the other kids play. She wanted to be like them.

Wilma's high school picture

Sports

Wilma worked hard to get stronger. By age 12, she did not use a crutch or a brace. Wilma was happy to play sports. Her brothers built a basketball hoop in their backyard. They taught Wilma how to play.

Wilma wanted to play basketball in high school. The coach wanted her sister on the team. Wilma's dad said both girls had to play. The coach agreed. Wilma became a star player!

Coach Ed Temple

Ed Temple was a college track coach. He saw Wilma play basketball. He thought Wilma could be a track star. He let Wilma practice with his college track team. Wilma practiced hard. She wanted to get better.

At first, Wilma was not a fast runner. Coach Temple showed her some special tricks to run faster.

FUN FACT

Wilma scored the most points in a state basketball championship.

Wilma and teammates train for the 1960 Olympics.

The Olympics

Wilma's hard work paid off. At age 16, she made it to the Olympics (uh-LIM-piks) for track and field. She won the bronze medal for the 100-meter relay race.

Wilma training for a race

Wilma and President John F. Kennedy

Wilma in a parade

No one thought Wilma's team would win a medal in the 1956 Olympics.

Wilma was proud of her bronze medal. But she wanted to win a gold medal. Wilma set goals. She worked hard for four years.

In 1960, Wilma went to the Olympics again. She ran in three races. She won every one. She was the first American woman to win three gold medals at one Olympics!

113

Wilma holding her college diploma

Wilma received an award with her hero, Jesse Owens, on the right.

A True Hero

After the 1960 Olympics, Wilma went to college. She became a teacher and a coach. Wilma won many awards, too. She was one of the first African American women to be honored for being a good athlete.

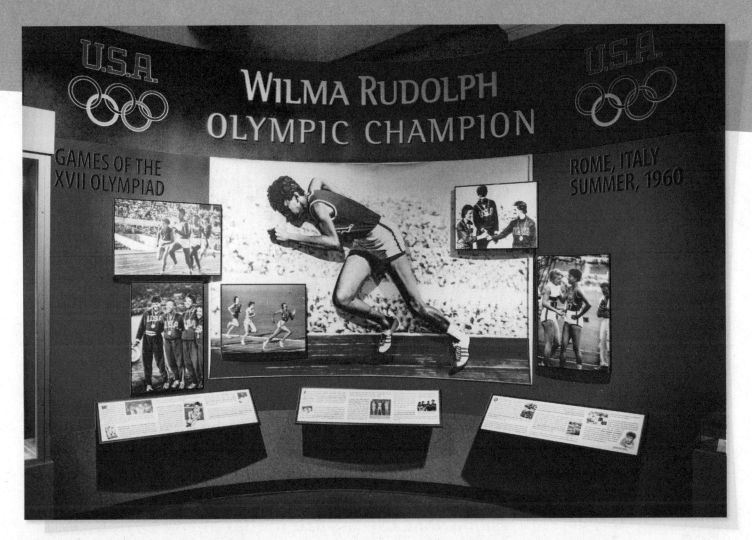

A display to honor Wilma is in a museum in Tennessee.

Wilma's success gave many women a chance to try new things. Sadly, Wilma died young on November 12, 1994. But her amazing work will never be forgotten.

FUN FACT

In 2004, the United States Postal Service created a stamp to honor Wilma.

Timeline

1940	Wilma Rudolph is born in Tennessee.
1944	Wilma is diagnosed with polio.
1952	Wilma learns to play basketball and walk without help from a crutch or a brace.
1956	Wilma wins the bronze medal at the Olympics.
1960	Wilma becomes the first American woman to win three gold medals at the Olympics.
1994	Wilma dies at the age of 54.

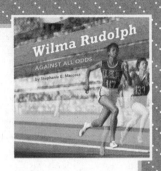

Use details from *Wilma Rudolph: Against All Odds* to answer these questions with a partner.

1. **Summarize** What did you learn about Wilma Rudolph's life? Use your own words to summarize the central idea and the relevant details in an order that makes sense.

2. What problems did Wilma face as a child?

3. Why do you think the author included a timeline on the last page? How can you use the timeline to find and understand information about Wilma Rudolph?

Listening Tip

Wait until your partner has finished speaking before asking a question or adding new information.

Write Advice

PROMPT What advice do you think Wilma Rudolph would give about believing in yourself? Use details from the text and photographs to explain your ideas.

PLAN First, make notes about the challenges Wilma Rudolph faced. Then make notes about her accomplishments.

Challenges	Accomplishments
Polio. She was born early. And her footand leg was wesd	She win 3 grad meto in one opik dtge lor and she go to presimeto in to

WRITE Now write the advice you think Wilma Rudolph would give about believing in yourself. Remember to:

- Include details from her life that support your ideas.

- Use words like *I believe* or *I feel*.

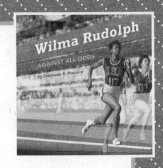

_____

_____

_____

_____

_____

_____

_____

_____

_____

_____

Prepare to Read

GENRE STUDY **Opinion writing** shows an author's thoughts, beliefs, or ideas. When you read *Great Leaders*, look for:

- what the author's opinion is
- reasons that support an opinion
- ways the author tries to make the reader agree with him or her

SET A PURPOSE As you read, think about the author's words. Then **evaluate,** or decide, which details are most important to help you understand the text.

POWER WORDS

politics

advice

earned

equal

Build Background: Having Opinions

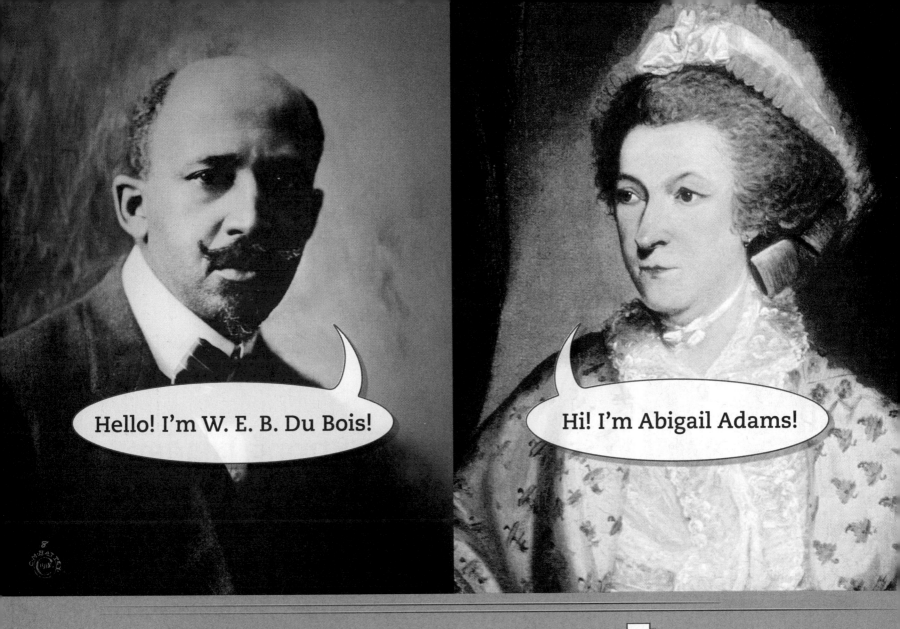

Great Leaders

The school newspaper asked two students to write their opinions about a great leader in history. Olivia chose Abigail Adams. Anthony chose W. E. B. Du Bois. Read both essays. What makes each person a great leader?

Hi! I'm Olivia!

Abigail and John Adams

ABIGAIL ADAMS:
Strong Woman, Strong Leader
by Olivia

Abigail Adams was a strong leader. She was focused on getting things done. I hope you will agree with me!

Abigail was the wife of our second president, John Adams. Many women didn't have a good education then. Abigail couldn't go to school when she was little because of illness. She was very smart, though. She learned things on her own. She studied history and politics.

When John was away, Abigail took care of her normal chores. She did John's chores, too! She even bought and sold land. Back then, only men did those types of jobs.

Abigail felt strongly about women's rights. As the United States was forming, she wrote a letter to John. She wanted him to tell the men to "remember the ladies." She felt women should help make the laws if they had to follow them.

Statue of Abigail Adams and her son

She also wanted girls to be able to go to public school like the boys. She and John often spoke about these things. He had respect for her ideas. Sometimes he would take her advice when making decisions. Because of this, some people called her "Mrs. President."

Boys and girls go to school together today.

As you can see, Abigail Adams did things that were unusual for women in her time. She helped her husband make decisions for the country. She talked about rights for women. She did jobs around the house that were usually done by men. Because of these reasons, I think Abigail Adams was a great example of a leader!

Statue of Abigail Adams in Boston

Hi! I'm Anthony!

W. E. B. DU BOIS
Was a Powerful Leader
by Anthony

W. E. B. Du Bois

I think W. E. B. Du Bois was an important leader in our country. He worked to change what he did not like. He wanted to help others, and he did. He also earned the respect of people around the world.

Harvard University

In 1895, W. E. B. Du Bois graduated from Harvard University, one of the best colleges in our country. He was the first African American to earn a special degree from there called a Ph.D. He led the way for others who wanted an education. While most people spend four years in college, W. E. B. Du Bois chose to stay longer. This shows he was a hard worker.

127

W. E. B. Du Bois had many jobs throughout his life. One of those jobs was a teacher. In a way, teachers are leaders. They set examples for how their students should act.

W. E. B. Du Bois

W. E. B. Du Bois felt strongly about people's rights. When he moved to Tennessee, he found that some people did not have the same rights as others. This made him sad and angry. He tried to fix the problem. W. E. B. Du Bois wrote papers and gave speeches about equal rights. He became a famous supporter of equal rights. Being active in the community made W. E. B. Du Bois a better leader. He knew how to reach people.

Mural of W. E. B. Du Bois
in Philadelphia

W. E. B. Du Bois expected a lot from himself and others. He was a good role model who showed others how to make positive changes. I think we should learn from his actions. If we do, we can all be leaders! Don't you agree?

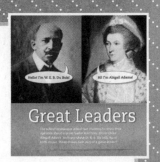

Great Leaders

Use details from *Great Leaders* to answer these questions with a partner.

1. **Evaluate** What are the most important details to remember about Abigail Adams and W. E. B. Du Bois? Look for clues in the text and pictures to help you decide.

2. Find two facts and two opinions about Abigail Adams. Then find two facts and two opinions about W. E. B. Du Bois. How do the opinions help you get to know the authors?

3. Why did the authors write these texts? What do they want to persuade you to think?

Talking Tip

Use your own words to explain details from the text. Complete the sentence below.

I read that _____ .

Write an Opinion

PROMPT Both Abigail Adams and W. E. B. Du Bois worked to make changes. How do you think their actions changed the lives of others? Use details from the words and photos to explain your ideas.

PLAN First, list the things that were important to Abigail Adams and W. E. B. Du Bois. Think about who they wanted to help.

Abigail Adams	W. E. B. Du Bois

WRITE Now write an opinion that explains how you think their actions changed the lives of others. Remember to:

- Use opinion words like *I think* or *I believe*.

- Use examples from their lives to support your ideas.

_____

_____

_____

_____

_____

_____

_____

_____

_____

_____

_____

Prepare to Read

GENRE STUDY **Informational text** is nonfiction. It gives facts about a topic. As you read *Who Are Government's Leaders?*, look for:

- captions with photos
- main topic and details
- headings that stand out

SET A PURPOSE As you read, **summarize** the text. Use your own words to retell the central idea and the relevant details in an order that makes sense.

POWER WORDS

troop

charge

solve

state

members

laws

capital

council

Build Background: What Is Government?

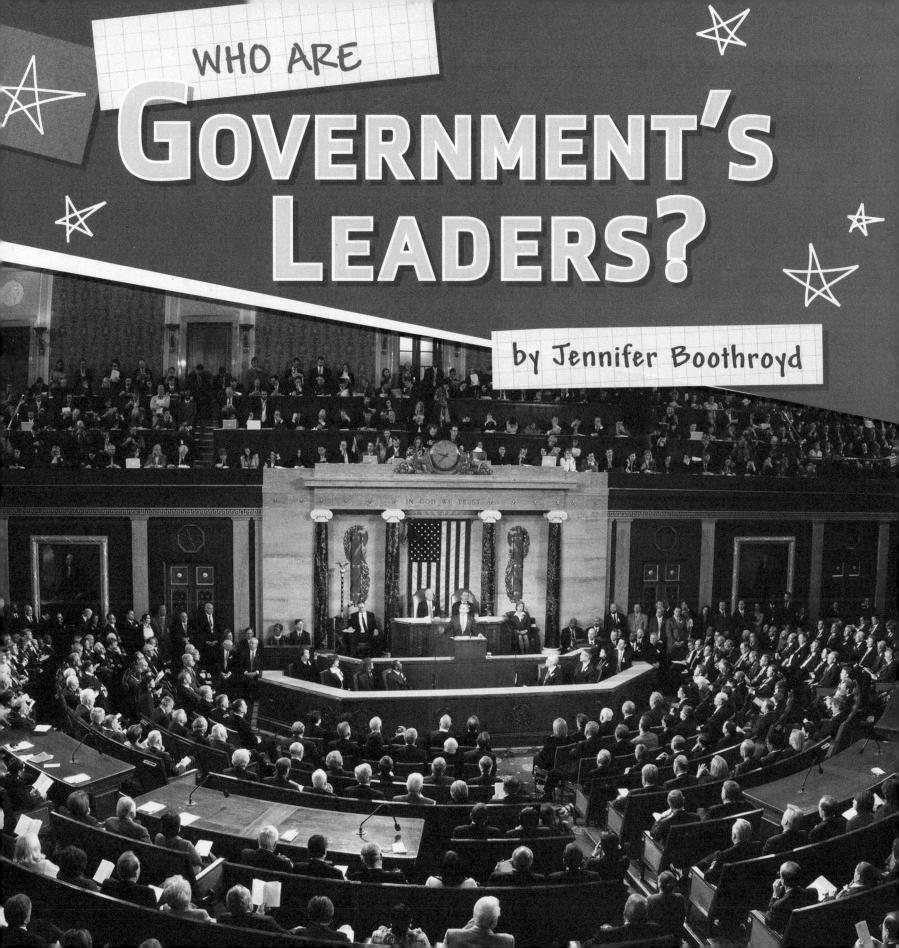

WHO ARE GOVERNMENT'S LEADERS?

by Jennifer Boothroyd

Government leaders write rules for us to follow.

This leader helps guide the scouts in his troop.

Who Is a Leader?

A leader is a person who is in charge of a group of people. Leaders try to help their groups and solve problems. Leaders try to work together and are good listeners, too.

Some leaders work in government. Government leaders help make rules. They make rules for our country, our state, and our city.

Our Country's Leaders

Our country's leaders work in Washington, D.C. The president leads our country, and **members** of Congress make **laws** for our country. The president and Congress work together.

Capitol Building in Washington, D.C.

Most governors are chosen every four years.

⭐ State Leaders

State leaders work in the state's capital city. People in each state choose a governor. The governor leads the state. The governor works with legislators, who make laws for their state.

City Leaders

A mayor is the leader of a city's government. The mayor works with the city council.

Citizens choose council members.

Good leaders make our country a
better place to live.

Use details from *Who Are Government's Leaders?* to answer these questions with a partner.

1. **Summarize** What did you learn about government leaders from this text? Use your own words to retell the central idea and the relevant details in an order that makes sense.

2. Why is being a good listener an important part of being a government leader?

3. What do you think is the most interesting part of being a government leader? What do you think is the most difficult part?

Listening Tip

Look at your partner as you listen. Nod your head to show you are interested.

Write a Help Wanted Ad

PROMPT A help wanted ad is an advertisement that appears in a newspaper when a job needs to be filled. It tells people what it takes to do that job. What would you write in a help wanted ad for a government leader? Use details from the words and photos to explain your ideas.

PLAN First, think about the skills that good government leaders need to have. Add them to the web.

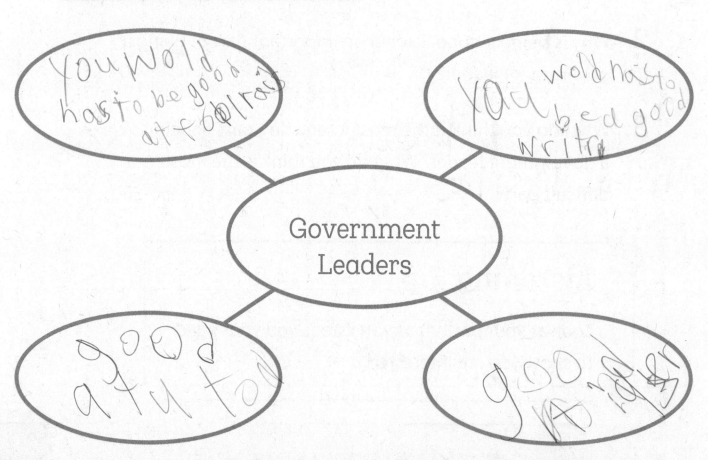

You wold hasto be good at foplrad

You wold hasto bed good writr

good a f u tal

good lader

Government Leaders

WRITE Now write a help wanted ad for a job as a government

leader. Remember to:

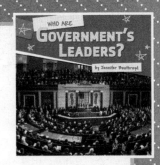

- Describe the skills a person will need to do a good job.

- Explain why this job is important.

Hlep watid-government
you must have thess
skils folofisn goodwridnd
goodatwtshe good tiger and daqum
es and good lisiner and
lisin to ante pelpes
ideus Beyamse we
nid more government

Prepare to View

GENRE STUDY ▸ **Videos** are short movies that give you information or something for you to watch for enjoyment. As you watch *Thomas Edison and the Light Bulb*, notice:

- how pictures, sounds, and words work together
- what the video is about
- information about the topic
- the tone or mood of the video

SET A PURPOSE ▸ One way to tell events is in **chronological order.** That means they are told in the order they happened. Pay attention to the order of events in the video. How does the order help you understand how the events are related?

Build Background: What Inventors Do

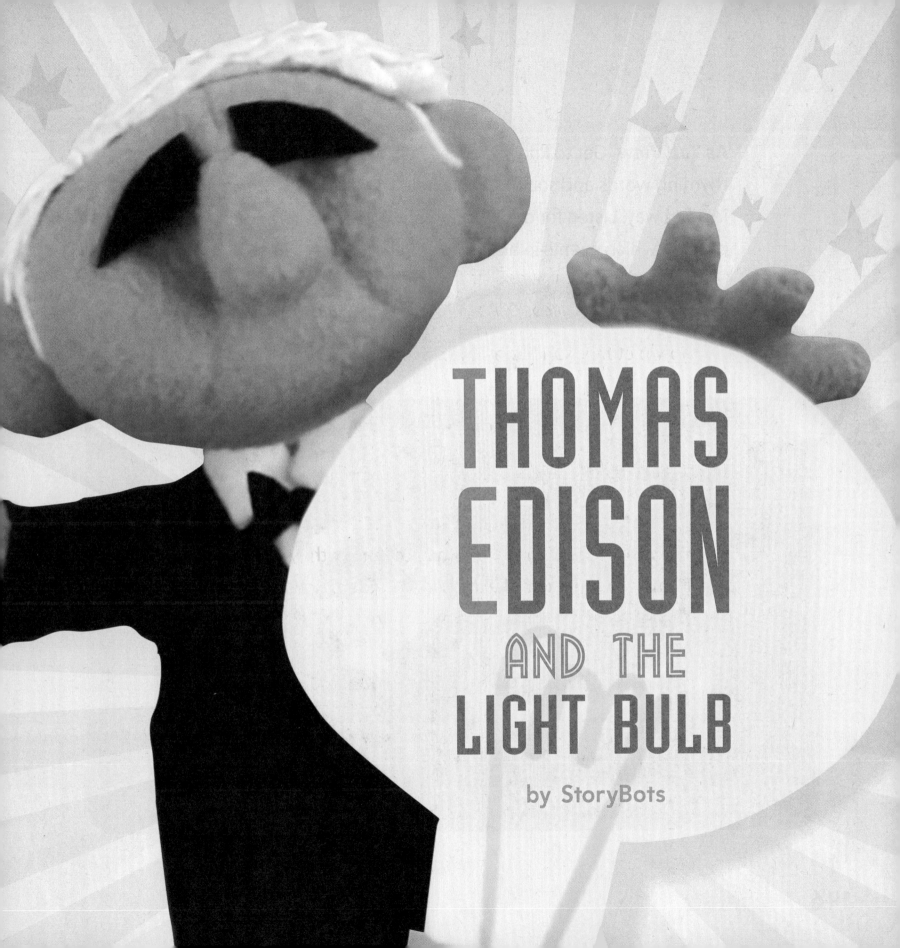

THOMAS EDISON AND THE LIGHT BULB

by StoryBots

As You View Get to know Thomas Edison! Think about how rhyming words and sound effects help to tell Mr. Edison's story in a fun way. Listen for details that help you understand the order in which events in his life happened.

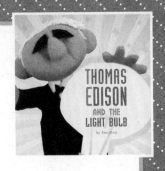

Turn and Talk

Use details from *Thomas Edison and the Light Bulb* to answer these questions with a partner.

1. Chronological Order What was the order of events that led to Edison's invention of the light bulb?

2. Why does the video show Edison throwing a plant onto a giant pile of plants? How does that help you understand how Edison felt about inventing?

3. What do Thomas Edison and Maya in *Going Places* have in common? What makes them both leaders?

Talking Tip

Ask to learn more about one of your partner's ideas. Complete the sentence below.

Please explain _____.

Let's Wrap Up!

? Essential Question

What are the qualities of a good leader?

Pick one of these activities to show what you have learned about the topic.

1. Interview a Leader

Think about the different leaders you read about in the texts. Which one would you most like to meet? Write five questions you would like to ask if you could interview that person.

Word Challenge

Can you use the word inspire in one of your questions?

2. Getting to Know Leaders

With a group, role-play a conversation between the leaders you read about. Have each group member be a different leader. Take turns introducing yourselves and describing what makes you a leader. Use details from the texts to explain your ideas.

My Notes

Weather Wise

"We'll weather the weather, whatever
the weather, whether we like it or not."

—Anonymous

Essential Question

How does weather affect us?

Get Curious Video

Words About Weather

Complete the Vocabulary Network to show what you know about the words.

climate

Meaning: **Climate** is the normal weather of a place.

Synonyms and Antonyms	Drawing
	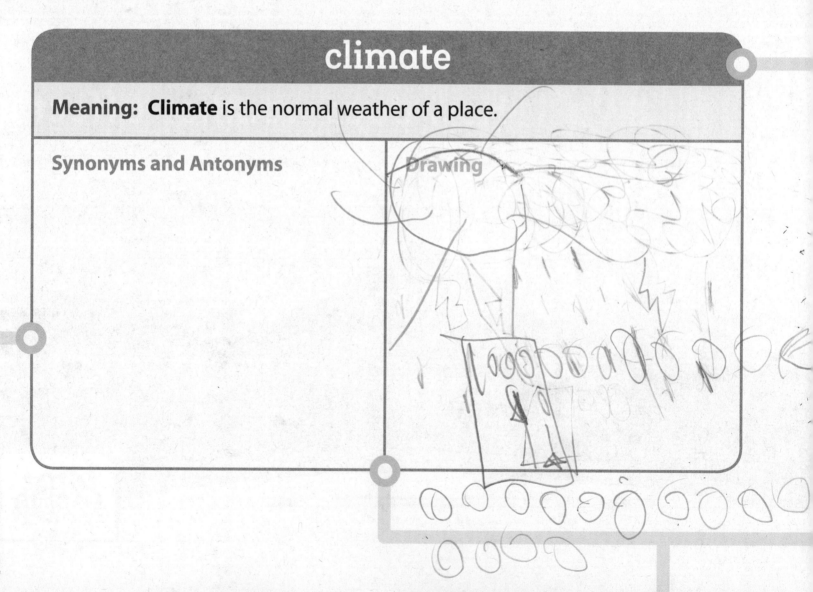

precipitation

Meaning: **Precipitation** is water that falls from the sky, such as rain, sleet, hail, or snow.

Synonyms and Antonyms	Drawing

temperature

Meaning: **Temperature** is how hot or cold a place is.

Synonyms and Antonyms	Drawing
	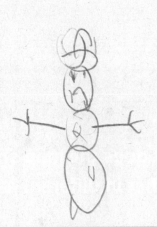

153

WEATHER THROUGH THE SEASONS

Weather is what the air is like outside. A weather map shows the weather in different places. Weather maps use symbols, shapes, and colors. Together, these things show us what the weather will be like.

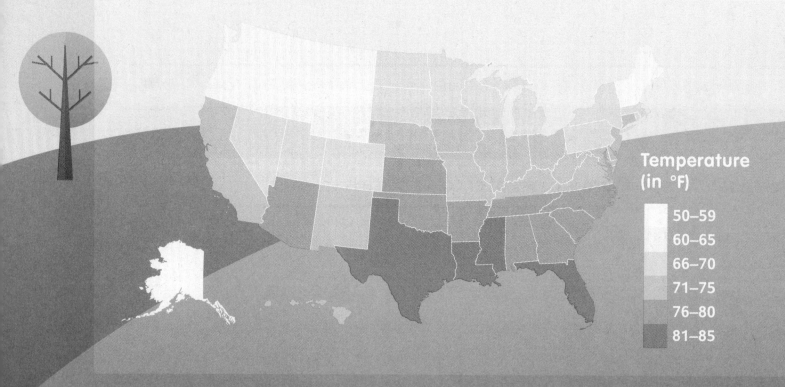

Average Summer Temperature

Temperature (in °F)

- 50–59
- 60–65
- 66–70
- 71–75
- 76–80
- 81–85

What does the map show you about summer weather in different parts of the country?

What do the words and pictures below tell you about winter weather?

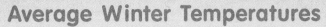

Average Winter Temperatures

State	Temperature (in °F)
Wisconsin	17.3
Ohio	25.3
Virginia	38.8
Texas	59.4
Florida	67.4

(in °F) 0 10 20 30 40 50 60 70

Average Yearly Snowfall

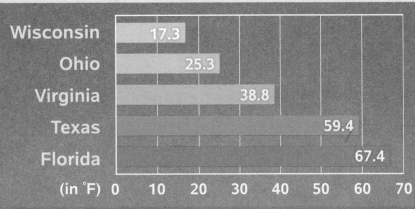

Inches of Snow

50 or more
25 to 50
12 to 25
1 to 12
0 to 1

How do summer and winter in your state compare to other parts of the country?

Prepare to Read

GENRE STUDY **Narrative nonfiction** gives facts about a topic, but it reads like a story. As you read *Wild Weather,* look for:

- information and facts about a real topic
- visuals such as maps or diagrams with text
- ways that visuals and words help readers understand the text

SET A PURPOSE Read to make smart guesses, or **inferences,** about things the author does not say. Use clues in the text and pictures to help you.

POWER WORDS

tough

pellets

predict

clings

funnel

occur

excess

damage

Meet Thomas Kingsley Troupe.

WILD WEATHER

by Thomas Kingsley Troupe

illustrated by Jamey Christoph

High up, along a mountain trail,
a hiker sat and folded an origami bird.

"It sure is sunny," she said. As she
held the bird high, a gust of wind lifted
the paper. The bird began to fly.

"Whoa, how did
it get so windy?"

Just then, the bird spotted
a duck flying nearby.

158

"Hey, there.
What's your name?"

The bird remembered
the hiker had said *sunny*.

"Sonny, I think."

"I'm Chuck. Nice to meet
you, Sonny. Say, I've got a real
problem. My wife, Natasha, is
missing. We were trying to fly
away from here."

159

"Why do you want to leave?" Sonny asked.
The mountain valley looked nice enough.

"Aren't you a bird? Most birds
fly south before winter. This wind
is making flying tough!"

"Where did all this
wind come from?"

WARM
AIR

COOL
AIR

"It's simple," he said. "The sun heats the land, making the air above it warm. The warm air rises. Cool air rushes to take the place of the warm air. And because Earth spins, wind can come from any direction."

"So, do you think the wind carried Natasha away?" Sonny asked.

"I hope not," Chuck cried. "She was right next to me, but then she disappeared!"

A drop of water struck Sonny's wing.

"Just what we need! It's raining! Fly underneath me, Sonny. I don't think wet paper is good for flying."

"Clouds and rain? How did they get here?"

"Check out this water cycle chart. It explains how clouds form and rain falls."

"Wow! That's pretty simple, really."

WATER CYCLE

The sun heats water on the ground, turning it into an invisible gas.

Gas rises, cools, and turns into water droplets.

Water droplets clump together to form clouds.

Water droplets combine and fall as rain.

"So rain is just a bunch of tiny droplets?" Sonny said. "That doesn't seem so bad."

"Normal rainstorms are fine. But thunderstorms can make lightning and heavy rain. When too much rain falls all at once, a flood can form."

"Whoa!"

"Hang on," Chuck yelled. "Hail is falling!"

"Hail?" Sonny chirped. "What's that?"

"Sometimes storm clouds called cumulonimbus clouds form. Water droplets in the highest parts of the cloud bounce around and freeze into ice pellets," Chuck said. "The pellets hit water droplets, and the hail gets bigger."

"And once the hail is too heavy, it falls?" Sonny asked.

"You got it," Chuck shouted. "Come on, let's head for the woods!"

"Isn't there any way to know when the weather will get wild?"

"There is! Meteorologists study and predict weather. They use tools to help them."

166

"Weather tools?"
Sonny asked. "Like what?"

"They have instruments to measure wind speed and direction," Chuck explained. "And radar to track rain and thunderstorms. Meteorologists even use satellites in outer space to track how and where the clouds move."

Sonny shivered. His papery body was growing cold.

"Natasha is lost, and it will snow any day now." Chuck quacked sadly.

"So what's the deal with snow?"

"It's a bit different than hail. The water vapor turns into an ice crystal. The ice crystal clings to other crystals and forms a snowflake."

"That doesn't sound so bad," Sonny said.

"If the ground and air are cold enough,
the snowflakes pile up and cover the ground,"
Chuck quacked. "The lakes freeze, and it's
tough for birds like us to find food."

"Oh! So that's why you fly south!"

"I'm not flying south without my wife! Natasha!" Chuck quacked. "Where are you?"

"How's the weather down south?"

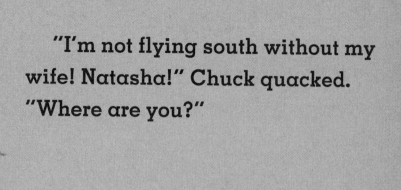

"It's much warmer. But the weather can get wild there too."

"What do you mean?" Sonny asked.

"Heat is measured in temperature," Chuck explained. "When the air is hot, the temperature is high. A low temperature means it's cool."

"That makes sense," Sonny said.

"Too much heat can hurt people, plants . . . even animals," Chuck quacked. "During a heat wave, the temperature and humidity stay high for two or more days."

"I wouldn't want to be stuck in one of those!" Sonny said.

Where was the worst heat wave on record? That would be 'down under.' The temperature in Marble Bar, Australia, was over 100 degrees Fahrenheit (38 degrees Celsius) for 160 days in a row in 1923. Hot days, mate!

"Where is Natasha? She couldn't have just disappeared!"

"What happened to those trees?"

"A tornado came through here years ago," Chuck said.

"What's a tornado?" Sonny asked.

"It's a funnel of wind that forms in the sky and wrecks what it touches on the ground," Chuck said. "Tornadoes form during a thunderstorm. They are more likely to occur over flat land."

"But how?" Sonny asked.

"When the wind in a storm changes direction, increases speed, and rises, it makes the air below it spin. Rising air pushes the spinning column of air downward until it's vertical. The spinning funnel of air speeds up, forming a tornado."

Tornadoes are usually determined to be weak, strong, or violent. The violent ones can have winds in excess of 200 miles (322 kilometers) per hour. They can destroy homes. Only 2 percent of tornadoes are violent.

"I had no idea weather could
be so scary," Sonny said.

"That's nothing. My
cousin Frank almost got
caught in a hurricane once."

"A hurricane? I'm afraid to ask!"

"A hurricane forms in summer or fall," Chuck said.
"It forms over an ocean and moves toward land."

"Does it make lots of wind like a tornado?" asked Sonny.

"Yes. Strong winds rotate around the 'eye' of the storm," said Chuck. "The spinning storm picks up energy from the warmth of the ocean. When it hits land, high winds and heavy rain can **damage** buildings."

The "eye" of a hurricane is the spot in the center of the storm. In the eye, the winds are light or calm, clouds break up and rain ends as the sky clears.

175

"Wow, all that dangerous weather scares me!" said Sonny.

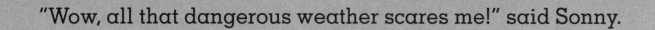

"Here's the thing, Sonny," Chuck said. "We can't control weather. But meteorologists can warn everyone when dangerous weather is coming, and we can prepare for it."

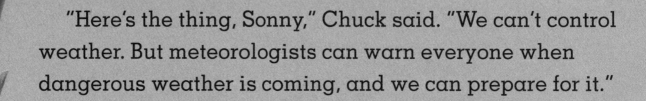

"Hey, Chuck. Is that your wife?"

"It is! Where were you, Natasha?"

"I went back for my sunglasses. I can't fly south without them!"

"Come with us, Sonny," Chuck said.

"I'd love to!" Sonny said. "But can I get some of those cool Sonny-glasses too?"

Use details from *Wild Weather* to answer these questions with a partner.

1. **Make Inferences** Why is a meteorologist's job important?

2. Look at the chart on page 163. How can you use the text and pictures to find and understand information about the water cycle?

3. In what ways is a hurricane like a tornado? How are they different? Use details from the text and pictures to explain your answer.

Talking Tip

Use details from the text to explain your ideas. Complete the sentence below.

I think _____ because _____.

Write an Opinion

PROMPT When you recommend a book, you try to persuade someone else to read it. What would you say to recommend *Wild Weather*? Think about what you liked best about the text and illustrations.

PLAN First, write three reasons you would give to persuade someone to read *Wild Weather*.

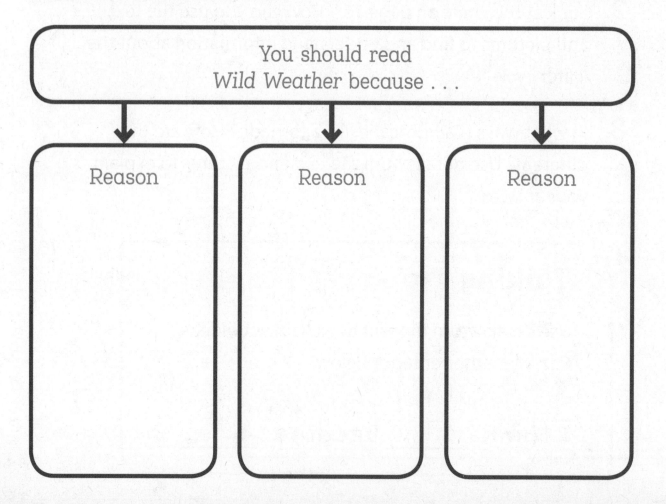

You should read
Wild Weather because . . .

Reason

Reason

Reason

WRITE Now write your opinion. Tell why you would recommend *Wild Weather*. Remember to:

- Use details that tell what readers will learn from *Wild Weather*.
- Use language that will make readers excited about reading it!

_____

_____

_____

_____

_____

_____

_____

_____

_____

_____

Prepare to Read

GENRE STUDY **Fantasies** are stories with made-up events that could not really happen. As you read *Cloudette,* look for:

- characters that are not found in real life
- a lesson the main character learns
- problems and solutions

SET A PURPOSE As you read, **make connections** by finding ways that this text is like things in your life and other texts you have read. This will help you understand and remember the text.

POWER WORDS

average

advantages

front

impressed

Meet Tom Lichtenheld.

Cloudette

by Tom Lichtenheld

Cloudette was a cloud.
A very small cloud.

Usually, Cloudette didn't mind being smaller than the average cloud.

Cloudette

Average Cloud

In fact, being small had lots of advantages.

Morning, small-fry.

Hey, shortcake!

Hi, pipsqueak!

Everyone called her cute little names.

Hey, guys, what's up?

Us!

Tee-hee!

That's nutty.

She had lots of little friends.

No matter how crowded it was, she could always find a good spot to watch fireworks.

183

She could sneak through tight spaces,

hide in small places,

Excuse me!

I can't find her anywhere!

Me either!

Tee-hee!

and she even had a special little space
that always made her feel cozy at night.

But once in a while, all the other clouds would
run off to do something big and important.

C'mon, Cloudette, join our
cold front. We're gonna make
a HUGE storm!

And make some
mighty rivers flow.

Yeah, we're gonna
water some crops.

No, thanks.
I'll just watch from here.

Cloudette could see them in the distance, doing
all sorts of important cloud things.

This made her want to do big and important things, too.

She wanted to make a garden grow.

She wanted to make
a brook babble.

She

wanted

to

make

a

waterfall

fall.

And she thought nothing
would be more fun than giving
some kids a day off from school.

187

One night, Cloudette lay awake wondering
what she could do that was big and important.

She thought maybe she could work
for the fire department.

Sorry, we just got a
brand-new pumper truck.

Or maybe they needed some help
down at the garden center.

Sorry, these plants
take TONS of water.

But nobody seemed
to need her.

Sorry, it's all
done by machines.

189

Cloudette was feeling blue.

The next day, there was a big storm in Cloudette's neighborhood.

The sky got dark, the rain came down like cats and dogs, and the wind blew harder than she'd ever seen wind blow before.

When the storm finally stopped, Cloudette realized she'd been blown far from her neighborhood.

She didn't know anyone here.

Hello.
Hi.
Howdy.
Howya doin'?

And they didn't seem eager to get to know her.

But pretty soon she was making new friends and seeing things she'd never seen before.

Then she heard something she'd never heard before.

ribbit

She looked down at what was supposed to be a pond,
but was really just a puddle of mud.

What happened to your pond, froggie?

*It dried up, and now it's more
like a puddle than a pond.*

This gave Cloudette an idea . . .

More like a
brainstorm,
actually.

She held her breath until she
started to puff up all over.

Then she turned a
nice blue-gray color.

She kept growing until
it looked like she was
ready to burst.

She shook her behind until it made a little
rumbling sound—not quite what you'd call
thunder, but enough to let people know they
might want to grab an umbrella.

Then she did what she'd wanted to do for ages.

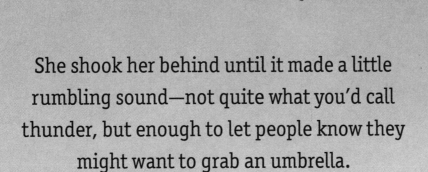

She

let

it

pour.

Cloudette rained on that little puddle until it grew into a big puddle.

And she kept on raining until that big puddle

grew into a perfect pond.

As soon as she stopped, frogs of every stripe (and spot) came jumping into the pond.

They all let out a big "Thank you!" in unison.

Cloudette was exhausted, but happy.

* "Thank you!" in Frog

Even the higher-ups were impressed,
which got her thinking . . .

I'll bet there are other
big and important things
a little cloud can do.

And off she went.

Use details from *Cloudette* to answer these questions with a partner.

1. **Make Connections** Think about a time when you were not big enough to do something you really wanted to do. How does that help you understand Cloudette's feelings?

2. How do the other characters in the story feel about Cloudette? What does this tell you about what she is like? Use details from the text and illustrations to explain your answer.

3. What does Cloudette learn about herself?

Listening Tip

Listen carefully. Make connections. How is what your partner is saying like other things you know?

Write the Next Chapter

PROMPT What will Cloudette do next? Use what you know about her to write about her next adventure. Look for details in the words and pictures to help you think of ideas.

PLAN First, draw a picture that shows what you think Cloudette will do next. Add a caption to describe what she is doing.

cloudette and itpete and

WRITE Now write a new adventure for Cloudette! Remember to:

- Look for details in the story that give clues about what Cloudette likes to do.
- Include details that describe what Cloudette is seeing, thinking, and feeling.

_____

_____

_____

_____

_____

_____

_____

_____

_____

_____

_____

Prepare to Read

GENRE STUDY **Informational text** is nonfiction. It gives facts about a topic. As you read *Get Ready for Weather*, look for:

- captions with art or photos
- headings, subheadings, or bold words that stand out
- how visuals and words help you understand the text

SET A PURPOSE Think carefully about the author's words as you read. Then **evaluate,** or decide, which details are most important to help you understand the text.

POWER WORDS
gusts
flash
supplies
layer

Build Background: What a Meteorologist Does

GET READY FOR WEATHER

by Lucy Jones

What's the Weather?

Take a look outside your window. What's the weather like today? It might be sunny or cloudy, rainy or snowy. One of the neat things about weather is that it's always changing. Temperatures can be warm or cold. Winds can be strong gusts or soft breezes. If it's rainy and chilly today, it could be sunny and warm tomorrow.

MONDAY

30°
HIGH 42°
LOW 23°

PARTLY CLOUDY

TUE	WED	THU	FRI	S
38°	31°	32°	37°	

Meteorologists tell us the weather.

People check the weather forecast to help plan their days. It tells if the weather will be rainy or sunny, hot or cold. Knowing what the weather will be helps people decide what to wear and do each day. If a big storm is on the way, the forecast explains what to expect and how to prepare.

Today's Forecast: Thunderstorms

Thunderstorms are storms that have rain, thunder, and lightning. Lightning can be very dangerous. Lightning can strike trees and telephone poles. The bright flash of lightning can be seen from very far away. Sometimes it can be seen from 100 miles away!

Thunderstorms usually happen in spring and summer.

If you hear the rumble of thunder, it is a good idea to <u>go inside right away.</u> Indoors is the best place to be during a thunderstorm. If you are outdoors, keep low to the ground. Also, be sure to stay away from trees.

Try This!

You can figure out how far lightning is from you! If you see lightning, start counting seconds until you hear thunder. For every 5 seconds you count, that's one mile away!

Today's Forecast: Blizzard

Blizzards are winter storms. They have very heavy snow and strong winds. It is hard to see in a blizzard. It can also be hard to walk because of the wind and the deep snow.

Blizzard Shopping

Stores get very crowded before a blizzard. People buy batteries and flashlights in case the electricity goes out. They buy extra food and water, too. Having the right **supplies** is one way to prepare for a storm.

After a blizzard, there is LOTS of shoveling to do! Snowplows work day and night to clear the roads. Neighbors help each other shovel sidewalks and driveways. School might be canceled for a few days. Kids can go sledding and build snowmen, but they better bundle up first! Wearing more than one layer of clothes will keep them warm in the frosty cold.

Today's Forecast: Sandstorm

Sandstorms happen when strong winds pick up sand. In the air, the sand forms into cloud shapes. In very strong winds, these sand clouds can grow to be 50 feet high! The winds can carry the sand for many miles. Sandstorms usually happen in dry, hot areas.

Sandstorms can form very quickly.

The best place to be during a sandstorm is indoors with the windows shut.

Being outside during a sandstorm is unsafe. Imagine being inside a swirling cloud of sand. It would be <u>very hard</u> to see. Sand could get in your eyes, nose, ears, and mouth. Covering your face with a cloth and wearing glasses is one way to protect yourself. Finding shelter and staying there until the storm is over is another way to stay safe.

Meteorologists use tools to help predict when and where storms will arrive. Knowing that a storm is coming can help you prepare. Storms can be dangerous, but they can be beautiful, too. Stay safe and enjoy the weather wherever you live!

Sometimes a rainbow appears after a rainstorm.

Keeping Pets Safe

When a big storm hits, pets need to be protected, too. Be sure your pets are indoors with you where it is safe and warm!

Turn and Talk

Use details from *Get Ready for Weather* to answer these questions with a partner.

1. **Evaluate** Which details in *Get Ready for Weather* help you understand how to get ready for a blizzard?

2. Look back at pages 208–209. What is the main idea of this section? What details tell more about it?

3. Compare and contrast *Get Ready for Weather* and *Wild Weather*. How are the texts alike? What are the most important differences between them?

Talking Tip

Complete the sentence to add to what your partner says.

My idea is _____.

Write Safety Tips

PROMPT What can you do to stay safe during different kinds of
weather? Use details from the words and pictures in *Get Ready
for Weather* to explain your ideas.

PLAN First, list some ways to stay safe during thunderstorms,
blizzards, and sandstorms.

Thunderstorm	Blizzard	Sandstorm
Than low and indoors. dot you uth if oa trees in sind r	Shoping and in doors sandstorm	Put grosse a cloth my ear oon oth

WRITE Now write five safety tips that will help people and pets stay safe during different kinds of weather. Remember to:

- Use verbs that tell people exactly what to do.
- Number each of your safety tips.

_____

_____

_____

_____

_____

_____

_____

_____

_____

Prepare to Read

GENRE STUDY > **Poetry** uses images, sounds, and rhythm to express feelings. As you read the poems in *Whatever the Weather*, look for:

- words that appeal to the senses
- words that make you think of powerful images or pictures
- words that are fun to say or that sound unique
- repetition of sounds, words, or lines

SET A PURPOSE > **Ask questions** before, during, and after you read to help you get information or understand the text. Look for evidence in the text and pictures to **answer** your questions.

POWER WORDS

splatter

rumble

slather

glide

covers

creep

slithering

shimmering

Build Background: Weather and Our Feelings

Whatever the Weather

A Collection of Poems

Weather

by Eve Merriam

Dot a dot dot   dot a dot dot
Spotting the windowpane.
Spack a spack speck   flick a flack fleck
Freckling the windowpane.

A spatter a scatter   a wet cat a clatter
A splatter a rumble outside.
Umbrella umbrella umbrella umbrella
Bumbershoot barrel of rain.

Slosh a galosh   slosh a galosh
Slither and slather and glide
A puddle a jump a puddle a jump
A puddle a jump puddle splosh
A juddle a pump aluddle a dump a
Puddmuddle jump in and slide!

221

Covers

by Nikki Giovanni

Glass covers windows
to keep the cold away

Clouds cover the sky
to make a rainy day

Nighttime covers
all the things that creep

Blankets cover me
when I'm asleep

223

Cloud Dragons

by Pat Mora

What do you see
in the clouds so high?
What do you see in the sky?

Oh, I see dragons
that curl their tails
as they go slithering by.

What do you see
in the clouds so high?
What do you see? Tell me, do.

Oh, I see *caballitos*
that race the wind
high in the shimmering blue.

Use details from *Whatever the Weather* to answer these questions with a partner.

1. **Ask and Answer Questions** What questions did you ask yourself about the poems before, during, and after reading?

2. Find places in "Weather" where the poet uses repetition. How do the sounds of the words help you picture what kind of weather she is writing about?

3. Compare and contrast the settings in "Covers" and "Cloud Dragons." How does each poem make you feel?

Listening Tip

Listen carefully. Think about the meaning of what your partner says.

Write a Weather Poem

PROMPT Which of the weather poems did you like best?
Choose a line, a phrase, or just a word from that poem. Use it to
write your own poem about weather.

PLAN First, write the words you chose from the poem on one
side of the chart. Then think of other words that describe that
kind of weather. Write them on the other side of the chart.

The Poem's Words	My Words
	dust is

WRITE Now put your words and the poem's words together to write a new poem about weather. Remember to:

- Think about how the words in your poem sound together.

- Use words that will help readers picture that kind of weather.

_____

_____

_____

_____

_____

_____

_____

_____

_____

_____

Prepare to View

GENRE STUDY ▶ **Videos** are short movies that give you information or something for you to watch for enjoyment. As you watch *Rain Cloud in a Jar,* notice:

- how pictures, sounds, and words work together
- information about the topic
- the purpose of the video

SET A PURPOSE ▶ Ask yourself what happens and why to find **cause and effect** connections in the video. A cause is something that makes something else happen. An effect is what happens because of the cause.

Build Background: Clouds

Rain Cloud in a Jar

by Sci-Tech Discovery

As You View Are you ready to make it rain? Watch the experiment. Observe what happens and why. Use the words and pictures to figure out how the steps in the experiment cause something to happen. How does this help you understand rain clouds?

Use details from *Rain Cloud in a Jar* to answer these questions with a partner.

1. **Cause and Effect** What causes the shaving cream cloud to get heavier? What is the effect?

2. Why is it important to add color to the water before you drip it on the shaving cream?

3. What does observing this experiment help you understand about weather?

Talking Tip

Add your own idea to what your partner says. Be sure to use polite language.

I like your idea. My idea is _____.

Let's Wrap Up!

(?) Essential Question

How does weather affect us?

....

Pick one of these activities to show what you have learned about the topic.

1. My Favorite Weather

What is your favorite kind of weather? Write your opinion. Use details from the texts and from your own experiences to explain what you like about it. Draw a picture to go with your writing.

2. Reporting the Weather

Be a TV weather reporter! Choose one kind of weather to report about. Use details from the texts to describe what you see, hear, and feel. Use your voice and body to show what it is like reporting in that kind of weather!

Word Challenge

Can you use the word precipitation in your weather report?

My Notes

Glossary

A

admire [ăd-mīr']   When you admire someone, you like and respect that person. I **admire** my friend for how he helps others.

advantages [ăd-văn'tĭj-ĕz]   Advantages are things that help put you ahead. Being a big brother has many **advantages**.

advice [ăd-vīs']   When you give advice, you tell people what you would do. My dad gives me good **advice**.

assured [ə-shoŏrd']   If you assured someone, you promised something would happen. The teacher **assured** us that the bus was on the way.

average [ăv'ər-ĭj, ăv'rĭj]   Something that is average is normal or usual. My cat is smarter than the **average** pet.

B

beamed [bēmd]   Someone who beamed gave a big smile. Caleb **beamed** when he read the funny story.

believe [bĭ-lēv']   When you believe something, you think it is true. I **believe** that it will rain today.

bind [bīnd]   When you bind something, you tie it up. He will **bind** the books together with string.

C

capital [kăp'ĭ-tl]   A capital is the city where the government meets to make laws. The government building is in the **capital** city.

charge [chärj]   When you are in charge, people follow your directions. Who is in **charge** of the group?

chore [chôr]   A chore is a job you must do. His **chore** is to take out the trash.

clever [klĕv′ər]   Someone who is clever is very smart. My dog is **clever** and knows many tricks.

climate [klī′mĭt]   Climate is the normal weather of a place. Some fruits grow best in a warm **climate**.

clings [klĭngz]   When something clings to something else, it sticks to it. Jane's hair **clings** to the balloon.

clue [kloo]   A clue is information that helps you find an answer. The open door was a **clue** that the lock needed to be fixed.

contraption [kən-trăp′shən]   A contraption is an object that looks strange and hard to use. Jim built an amazing flying **contraption**.

council [koun′səl]   A council is a group of people elected to lead. The members of the **council** will work together to make a decision.

covers [kŭv′ərz]   Something that covers something else goes over it. Snow **covers** the yard during winter.

cozy [kō′zē]   A place that is cozy is comfortable. The fireplace made the room very **cozy**.

creep [krēp]   When things creep, they move quietly and slowly. I saw the cat **creep** closer to the bird.

D

damage [dăm′ĭj]   When you damage something, you cause harm to it. The storm could **damage** the old tree.

dashed [dăsht]   If you dashed, you ran quickly. My dad **dashed** out the door to get to work on time.

disturb [dĭ-stûrb′]   When you disturb someone, you bother that person. Please do not **disturb** me while I'm sleeping.

E

earned [ûrnd]   If you earned something, you got what you worked for. We **earned** money by selling lemonade.

equal [ē′kwəl]   Something that is equal is the same amount as something else. She divided the pie into **equal** pieces.

exactly [ĭg-zăkt′lē]   When things are exactly alike, they are the same in every way. My brother and I look **exactly** alike.

excess [ĭk-sĕs′, ĕk′sĕs′]   An excess of something is more than is needed. Please remove any **excess** glue from the paper.

F

flash [flăsh]   A flash is a sudden burst of light. The **flash** of lightning was very bright.

front [frŭnt]   A cold front is where cold air meets warm air. A cold **front** will bring snow showers.

fulfill [fool-fĭl′]   When you **fulfill** something, you make it happen. I always **fulfill** a promise.

funnel [fŭn′əl]   A funnel has a wide circle at the top and a short, thin tube at the bottom. She poured the mixture into the **funnel**.

G

glide [glīd]   Things that glide move smoothly and easily. My new skates help me **glide** over the ice.

gusts [gŭsts]   Gusts are short, strong rushes of wind. **Gusts** of wind kept blowing my umbrella inside out.

H

hobbled [hŏb′əld]   If you hobbled, you walked in a slow, uneven way. The boy **hobbled** home after he hurt his leg.

honored [ŏn′ərd]   When people are honored, they are praised for what they have done. Laila was **honored** for her volunteer work.

I

impressed [ĭm-prĕst′]   If you are impressed, you like something a lot. She **impressed** us with her singing.

inspire [ĭn-spīr′]   When people inspire you, they give you new ideas. I want to **inspire** others to be good leaders.

intent [ĭn-tĕnt′]   Someone who is intent is set on doing something. The cat was **intent** on staring at the birds.

J

jealous [jĕl′əs]   If you are jealous, you feel angry because you want what someone else has. I felt **jealous** when Emma won first place.

journey [jûr′nē]   A journey is a trip from one place to another. The map helped Cheri plan her **journey**.

L

laws [lôz]   Laws are rules that people must follow. Our country has many important **laws**.

layer [lā′ər]   If you have on more than one layer of clothing, you are wearing several things on top of one another to keep warm. I always put on more than one **layer** of clothes on snowy days.

M

members [mĕm′bərz]   Members are people who belong to a group. The other **members** of government welcomed the new senator.

moral [môr′əl, mŏr′əl]   A moral is a lesson in a story. The **moral** of the story is to keep trying.

N

narrow [năr′ō]   Something that is narrow is thin and has little space. It was hard for cars and bikes to fit together on the very **narrow** street.

O

occur [ə-kûr′]   When things happen or take place, they occur. The graduation party will **occur** as soon as the ceremony is over.

P

pause [pôz]   If you pause, you stop what you are doing for a short time. The speaker will **pause** so we can ask questions.

peered [pîrd]   If you peered, you looked closely. Sofi and Diana **peered** into the microscope at the drop of pond water.

pellets [pĕl′ĭts]   Pellets are tiny balls of something. Savannah brushed her pet rabbit and gave it some food **pellets**.

pioneer [pī′ə-nîr′]   When you pioneer something, you are the first person to do it. Astronauts help us **pioneer** new ways of exploring outer space.

plain [plān]   A plain is a flat piece of land with few trees. We saw beautiful flowers on the **plain**.

pleasure [plĕzh′ər]   Pleasure is a feeling of happiness or joy. It is always a **pleasure** to see you.

politics [pŏl′ĭ-tĭks]   Politics is the work done by people in government. Helping people in his community was his favorite part of working in **politics**.

precipitation [prĭ-sĭp′ĭ-tā′shən] Precipitation is water that falls from the sky, such as rain, sleet, hail, or snow. The weather report shows a strong chance of **precipitation**.

precise [prĭ-sīs']   Something that is precise is exact and correct. She gave us **precise** directions to the park.

predict [prĭ-dĭkt']   If you predict something, you say it will happen before it does. I **predict** that it will be sunny tomorrow.

R

rare [râr]   Something that is rare does not happen often. It is **rare** for my brother to clean up his room.

rattled [răt'ld]   Something that rattled made many short, shaking noises. The coins **rattled** in my pocket.

relate [rĭ-lāt']   If you relate to someone, you know how the person feels. I can **relate** to how the character in this story is feeling.

relay [rē'lā]   A relay is a team race where each member runs one part of it. It takes teamwork to win a **relay** race.

replica [rĕp'lĭ-kə]   A replica is an exact copy of something. Each cookie was a **replica** of the other.

respond [rĭ-spŏnd']   When you respond, you answer in some way. I do not know how to **respond** to your question.

rumble [rŭm'bəl]   A rumble is a long, booming noise. We heard a **rumble** of thunder.

S

sense [sĕns]   Something that makes sense is easy to understand. It makes **sense** to practice before the big game.

shimmering [shĭm'ər-ĭng]   Something that is shimmering is shining. The silver confetti was **shimmering** in Jem's hands at the party.

239

slather [slă*th*′ər]   If you slather something, you put a lot of it over something else. Let me **slather** this sunscreen on your face before we go to the beach.

slithering [slĭ*th*′ər-ĭng]   If something is slithering by, it is sliding past. We saw a snake **slithering** through the grass.

solve [sŏlv, sôlv]   When you solve a problem, you find an answer to it. I want to **solve** this math problem.

speech [spēch]   A speech is a talk you give to an audience. My friend gave an inspiring **speech** after she won an award for her good citizenship.

splatter [splăt′ər]   When things splatter, drops fall out of them. If you aren't careful, paint will **splatter** on the floor.

state [stāt]   A state is an area of land that is part of a country and has its own government. We will visit the **state** of Florida.

steaming [stēm′ĭng]   If something is steaming, it is very hot. The soup was **steaming**, so we had to wait a few minutes for it to cool.

success [sək-sĕs′]   Success is when you finish something you worked hard to do. Our talent show was a big **success**.

superb [soo-pûrb′]   Something that is superb is the very best. The celebration we had for my grandfather's birthday was **superb**!

supplies [sə-plīz′]   Supplies are the things people need to be ready for something. I have all the **supplies** I need for the storm.

T

tackled [tăk′əld]   If you tackled someone, you pushed the person to the ground. He **tackled** the player with the football.

temperature [tĕm′pər-ə-cho͝or′, tĕm′pər-ə-chər, tĕm′prə-cho͝or′, tĕm′prə-chər]   Temperature is how hot or cold a place is. How cold is the **temperature** today?

thrilled [thrĭld]   When you are thrilled, you are very excited. The kids were **thrilled** to go camping.

tough [tŭf]   If something is tough to do, it is difficult or challenging. It was a very **tough** choice so we decided to get both kittens.

troop [tro͞op]   A troop is a group of people who belong to a club. My friends and I are in the same girls' **troop** at school.

V

version [vûr′zhən]   A version is a different or changed form of something. We played a new **version** of the game.

Index of Titles and Authors

Acknowledgments

"Cloud Dragons" from *Confetti: Poems for Children* by Pat Mora. Text copyright © 1996 by Pat Mora. Reprinted by permission of Lee & Low Books Inc.

Cloudette by Tom Lichtenheld. Copyright © 2011 by Tom Lichtenheld. Reprinted by arrangement with Henry Holt Books for Young Readers.

Web/Electronic Versions: *Cloudette* by Tom Lichtenheld. Copyright © 2011 by Tom Lichtenheld. Reprinted by arrangement with Henry Holt Books for Young Readers. CAUTION: Users are warned that this work is protected under copyright laws and downloading is strictly prohibited. The right to reproduce or transfer the work via any medium must be secured with Henry Holt and Company.

"Covers" From *The Sun Is So Quiet* by Nikki Giovanni. Text copyright © 1996 by Nikki Giovanni. Reprinted by permission of Henry Holt Books for Young Readers.

Going Places by Peter and Paul Reynolds. Text copyright © 2014 by Peter H. Reynolds and Paul A. Reynolds. Illustrations copyright © 2014 by Peter H. Reynolds. Reprinted by permission of Atheneum Books For Young Readers, an Imprint of Simon & Schuster Children's Publishing Division, and Pippin Properties, Inc.

How to Read a Story by Kate Messner. Illustrated by Mark Siegel. Text copyright © 2015 by Kate Messner.

Illustrations copyright © 2015 by Mark Siegel. Reprinted by permission of Chronicle Books LLC.

"Weather" from *Catch a Little Rhyme* by Eve Merriam. Text copyright © 1966, renewed © 1994 by Eve Merriam. Reprinted by permission of Marian Reiner.

Excerpt from *Who Are Government's Leaders?* by Jennifer Boothroyd. Text copyright © 2016 by Lerner Publishing Group, Inc. Reprinted by permission of Lerner Publications Company, a division of Lerner Publishing Group, Inc.

Wild Weather by Thomas Kingsley Troupe, illustrated by Jamey Christoph. Copyright © 2014 by Picture Window Books, a Capstone imprint. Reprinted by permission of Capstone Press Publishers.

Wilma Rudolph: Against All Odds by Stephanie E. Macceca. Text copyright © 2011 by Teacher Created Materials, Inc. Reprinted by permission of Teacher Created Materials, Inc.

Credits

Credits